AUTISM GOES TO COLLEGE
JEFF'S COMING OF AGE STORY

DR. SHARON A. MITCHELL

Other books in the series:

Autism Goes to School
Autism Runs Away
Autism Belongs
Autism Talks and Talks
Autism Grows Up
Autism Goes to College - Jeff's Coming of Age Story
Autism Questions Parents Ask
Autism Questions Teachers Ask

This is a work of fiction, a figment of the author's imagination. Any resemblance to real people or events is coincidental. The story is for entertainment and information purposes only. The author assumes no responsibility for the strategies and suggestions described.

Copyright © 2020 Sharon A. Mitchell
All rights reserved.
ISBN 978-1-988423-166
ISBN 978-1-988423-15-9 (ebook)

CHAPTER 1

"It's not going to work." Mel was adamant.

"He'll be fine." Her mother dismissed her concerns.

"He's going to crash and burn and if you don't see that, you're fooling yourself."

"Melanie Nicols watch your mouth. You know that your brother's a genius when it come to that computer stuff."

"He might have a gift in that area but what you have planned just won't work. He cannot move away from home and succeed at university, at least not right now. He's not ready. You've done nothing to prepare him."

"Nonsense. He's twenty. That is older than you were when you started college. That's older than most freshmen."

"But Jeff is not most freshmen. He's autistic."

"Shush, Mel. Of course, he isn't. He has Asperger's Syndrome."

"Same difference."

"You know as well as I do, that it's not the same thing. A diagnosis of Asperger's has much better outcomes."

"Yeah, well, it has the possibility of a more independent outcome *if* the person has received the necessary help."

Hands on her hips, Doreen Nicols said, "Are you suggesting that your father and I did not help Jeff? Why, we helped both you and your brother to the best of our ability."

Mel relented. "Mom, I know that you did your best and that Jeff is smart. But he's just not ready to live on his own, plus cope with university life at the same time. Why couldn't he stay home and take some college courses locally? You know, sort of ease into things."

"He's been accepted into one of the best tech schools around, that's why. His talents can't go wasting with just mediocre training."

MEL RETURNED to washing the pots and pans, while her mother loaded the dishwasher. Jeff stumbled in, scratching his stubbly chin. He wore low slung sweatpants and a t-shirt better suited to the rag pile. He stretched, elbow joints popping. "What's for lunch?"

"Breakfast was over five hours ago, and lunch finished half an hour ago," his sister informed him.

"Mel, enough." Their mother shot her a look.

"There's plenty of food." She started pulling covered bowls from the refrigerator. "We had roast pork with mashed potatoes, peas and applesauce for lunch. I can heat that up again or make you a fried egg sandwich."

"Are there any of those calzones we had for supper last night?"

"I froze the extras. I'll just run down to the freezer and get you a couple. It won't take long to bake them." To Mel she added, "Please turn the oven on to 375."

"Mom, this is exactly what I'm talking about," Mel protested.

Doreen hesitated on her way down the stairs. "What? You'll deny your brother some food?"

"No, it's the catering I object to. How is this going to work when he's away at school?"

"I'll have to fatten him up whenever he comes home, the same as I would for you."

MEL SHOOK HER HEAD. She turned to her brother. "Jeff, you have to learn to do some of these things for yourself."

"What are you on at me for? Just because you and mom are fighting again, doesn't mean you're going to draw me into it."

"We're not fighting."

Mel continued scrubbing pots, perhaps with a bit more vigor. Finally, she said, "You could at least have offered to help."

"Help with what?"

"These dishes for a start."

"I didn't know you needed help. You always do them just fine by yourself, and you didn't ask me to help. How can I know if you don't say anything?"

Mel's eyes rolled so far up that Jeff wondered how she could see what she was scrubbing.

MORE SLOWLY THAN she had descended, their mother puffed her way past the top of the basement stairs. "It'll just be a few minutes, Jeff." She set the calzones into the warmed toaster oven, then bustled around her kitchen. One at a time, she centered a place mat, then a plate, cutlery, and a water glass in front of Jeff. Mel watched with her arms crossed.

From experience, Jeff knew that more was coming. "What?" he asked.

"Don't you think you could have done some of that yourself?" said his sister.

"Nonsense," Doreen interrupted. "He knows I love doing things for him, and soon he won't be here for me to spoil." She patted her son's shoulder.

"Spoil is right," muttered Mel. Then, to Jeff she asked, "Who do you think is going to do stuff like this for you at college?"

Jeff's frown confirmed Mel's worries. He had not thought about this.

"Don't let a little thing like that worry you, Jeffy. It'll

all work out. You'll see." She continued. "And maybe you'll make a nice friend."

"I don't need a friend."

His mom's reassurance did not alleviate Jeff's scowl. He turned to Mel.

She mouthed, "Later."

MEL SIGHED as she walked back through the kitchen, noting the crumbs, dirty plate, knife and fork and half-finished cup of coffee where Jeff had been sitting. For a few seconds she debated clearing the things away herself or calling Jeff to do it. She opened the basement door, hollering, "Jeff! Get up here a minute, please."

As Jeff started up the stairs, their mother bustled in, snatching up Jeff's leavings.

"Yeah, what do you want, Mel?" Jeff asked.

"I thought you could clean up your own dishes."

Jeff looked puzzled at the spot where he had eaten. "They're gone."

"Right," his sister said. "Someone else had to do it."

"That's mom's job. It's her kitchen and she doesn't want anyone messing in it."

"Exactly right," Doreen agreed. "My kitchen, my rules."

"Well, how come you expect me to clean up after myself?" Mel was sure that was not a whine creeping into her voice. "And, don't you dare say because I'm a girl and Jeff's a boy."

"Dear, I would not say that; it would be sexist, and

you know I don't hold with that sort of thing. You and Jeff are two different people. I *like* to do things for him."

Then she noticed how Mel's chin jutted out. She rubbed her daughter's shoulder. "There, there. You know that we love you both equally, but you are two different people. You are so capable and Jeff, well..."

"Hey!" interrupted Jeff.

"You kids. You'd squabble like this when you were children and pull me into it." She faced her daughter. "You are always so fiercely independent, and Jeff likes me to do things for him and I like to do those things. It's a system we've worked out while you've been away at school and we like it fine."

Mel tried again. "But it's a system that can't be sustained. Jeff's moving away in a week. How is this going to work for him? He's not used to doing anything for himself. Are you planning on moving with him?"

"Mel, you do worry a lot, don't you dear?" With that Doreen left the room.

JEFF WAITED until Doreen was gone. "So, you're home, what a week, and already you and mom are going at it? We did manage just fine while you were gone, you know. You don't have to come in and make us all over."

Mel sighed. "Jeff let's go for a walk. I'll tell you about what's bugging me."

They headed for the park, the place they had used as a refuge since childhood.

"I'm worried about you, Jeff."

"Me? It sounded like it was mom you had the problem with."

"Well, it is, sort of. I think that some of what she is doing is going to cause you problems." They headed for the swings and, out of habit, each took a seat on their usual spots.

"Pretty quick you'll be heading off to college, moving away and living on your own in a dorm."

"Yeah, so? I know that."

"I'm not sure you know all that it entails." She waited a couple minutes, watching the Canada geese float in the pond.

"Mel, I can handle it. I might have Asperger's and I might have dropped out of high school, but I'm not dumb. I can do it."

She looked at her younger brother. "No, you certainly aren't dumb; you might be one of the smartest people I have met. But that's not what I'm talking about. You might have brain power, but when it comes to life skills, you've never had to learn many. At home, mom looks after everything and living on your own is going to come as a rude shock, with all the things you'll have to do for yourself."

"Do you think I can't figure that out? You did."

"Yeah, I did, but it was different for me. I had lots of experience doing things before I ever left home."

"Like what?"

"Like today at lunch. You got up hours after

everyone else had finished not only breakfast but lunch as well. You just announce that you're hungry and food magically appears for you. College won't be like that."

"No, I'll walk into the cafeteria and other mom-like creatures will have the food all spread out. It won't be like home, but I'll have more choice."

"There's that, yes. But when you're done, you don't just walk away. You'll be expected to pick up your plate and tray and put your used things on a conveyor someplace. There will be no mom to clean up after you."

"I think I figured that out already. Actually, any moron would."

"Jeff, that's just an example and the tip of the iceberg of all the things you'll have to do for yourself that you're not used to doing."

"Tip of the iceberg. Well, I don't plan on taking any geography classes, so we don't need to worry about that, and I doubt that they'll keep the cafeteria that cold."

Mel pushed off with her feet and swung higher, throwing her head back so that her hair swished nearly to the ground. She closed her eyes and swung for a bit. She tried a different tack.

"College was hard for me. Much as I wanted to be there, I thought about quitting a number of times, especially during that first semester. Everything was so different. I didn't know anyone. Things seemed to come at me so fast and furious for a while that I felt like I was in over my head."

"But you didn't quit."

"No, it got better. I got used to things, learned how to manage my time and my assignments and well, my life. But it wasn't easy, and I know it was the same for lots of other students."

"And you think that is going to happen to me?"

She nodded, then stopped her swing so she could turn to face him. Taking a deep breath, she said, "I think it might be even harder for you. I'd had more experience than you before I left home about things like looking after myself, mixing with other people and organizing things."

Jeff wound the chains of his swing, spinning himself the way he did as a child. "I think about that, too." He looked up. "I'm scared, Mel. I remember what it felt like in high school, like I was suffocated and drowning in this sea of kids who didn't get me, and I didn't get them. The work I could do, well, when I wanted to, but being around those students was more than I could take." He spun and unwound some more. "But it's supposed to be different in college. The kids are adults now and more mature. Those ones who knew me in high school and made my life hell won't be there. No one will know me or remember that I'm that geeky kid it's okay to pick on." His eyes pleaded with his sister to assure him that it would be different this time.

Mel shook her head. "I'm not sure."

At Jeff's look, she hurried on. "I mean, I'm not sure about a lot of it. Yeah, the stuff you went through in high school likely won't be the same. Yeah, there are still jerks in college, just like there are in the workplace and everywhere, but people usually grow up. College students are older. They don't have those same adolescent needs to prove themselves, or at least not as much. On campus, there won't be students who have grown up with each other all their lives. Most of them will be strangers. They come alone and new to campus, looking to make friends. So, I think you'll find them a more diverse group and more accepting of everyone."

"But I'll still need to watch out for the jerks."

"Sadly, yes. You will always encounter some, but most of the students won't be like that."

"I don't really care if I'm buddy-buddy with people. That's not why I'm going to school. I want to learn."

"That's an advantage of college. Most people are there to learn. And since there are so many people on campus and in each class, mainly first year classes, it is easier to be anonymous among the crowd. Some people just go to class, mind their own business, do their work and move on to the next class."

"That's what I'll do."

Mel nodded. "Yes, and that could work. You would be missing out on some of the other positive things about campus, though. Some people make good friends during these years, with people who have similar interests."

"Mel, do you really see that happening with me?"

"You could join some groups. There are all sorts of interest clubs on campus, some that focus on computers and programming that you might probably like."

"Right." Although Jeff had had a hard time catching on to sarcasm as a teen, he had perfected its use now.

Mel scuffed the dirt with her toe.

"Is it just you and mom getting on each other's

nerves, or is there something else bugging you about me going to college?" Jeff asked.

"Okay. Here's what I think. You usually don't like surprises, right?"

Jeff nodded.

"You like routine and knowing what to expect."

"Yeah. So?"

"Mom thinks she and dad are going to drive you to college next week, drop you off at the dorm and everything will be fine. Have you even looked at the place?"

"I looked at it on Google Maps."

"And you think that's good enough?"

He shrugged.

"I've seen you in new places. When you go to a mall that's new to you, you freeze inside the door. The lights, the noise, the crowds all seem to unnerve you."

"So, I like to shop in places I know. That way I can get in, get what I want, then get out."

"Well, you're not going to know this campus. Believe me, it is crowded, and worse during class changes. Even the cafeterias are noisy and crowded. You usually don't like crowds."

"I'll go eat after the crowd leaves."

"That will work some of the time, although you'll still need to be there within certain hours. But it's not just the cafeteria. There will be tens of thousands of students hurrying to get to their next class in the ten-minute break. Some of your classes will be in different buildings. You're not a fan of crowds; the noise, and moving bodies can be confusing; it's worse if you are not sure where you are going, plus you don't like people brushing against you."

Jeff almost visibly shuddered. "Maybe I'll only take classes that are in non-crowded areas."

"It doesn't work like that."

"So, what am I supposed to do, Mel? Not go? It sounds like there is a lot about the place that I will hate anyway."

"I have some ideas." She stood up. "Let's go. I promised Mom I'd pick up some things for her at the supermarket before she starts supper. Wanna come?"

JEFF TRUDGED along about three paces behind Mel. She was used to it - sort of. When Jeff was in certain moods or when he was in a building with bright fluorescent lights, he seemed to go somewhere else in his mind. Although his footsteps followed hers down the produce aisle, she didn't think he saw any of the fruits or vegetables they passed. She held up two apples. "Jeff, which variety to you prefer?"

"Ah, what? Sorry Mel, I wasn't listening. What is it?"

"I asked which type of apple you like better."

"*That's* what you called me over here to ask? Who cares? An apple is an apple. I'm busy thinking."

Knowing it was of no use trying to engage her brother in a discussion about fruit, Mel left him to his own thoughts. Out of the corner of her eye, she watched him as she sorted through a pile of navel oranges. He remained over by the celery and lettuce section, oblivious to a woman trying to reach by him for a head of romaine, or of the overhead spray that came on, slightly wetting the sleeve of his shirt.

Mel knew that she was partly responsible for Jeff's reverie. She may have laid it on a bit too heavily about what college might be like, but he needed to know. It was NOT going to be easy for him and even less so if he was not prepared. She watched him sinking deeper into himself, and knew it was probably due to the picture she painted. Well, better to work through it now than when he arrived on campus alone, with the stressors of dorm life, and class assignments.

JEFF KEPT his hands behind his back, his fingers worrying one another. He realized that a woman was staring at him after saying, "Excuse me" quite loudly. This was likely not the first time she had said it. "Oh, sorry," he apologized and moved closer to the dairy and juice section. No one was nearby and there was room to pace a bit.

Jeff walked back and forth, his head down and his fingers moving. Mel came by, searching for the freshly squeezed orange juice. "Did you say something, Jeff? I didn't catch it, but I saw your lips moving."

Jeff startled. "Ah, no. I was just thinking to myself." He looked at his sister. "Are we about ready to get out of here?"

Mel gestured to her nearly empty cart. "We just got here. Mom gave me quite a list of things she wants us to pick up. Here." She tore the paper in half and held out the bottom part of the list to Jeff. "If we each get half of the stuff, it'll go much quicker."

If she'd pushed a hissing snake toward his hands, Jeff would not have recoiled faster. "Geez, Mel, no. We need to get out of here. I'm not in the mood for shopping, and there are too many people."

Mel looked at the mid-weekday afternoon group of shoppers. Compared to the right-after-work crowds, this was nothing. She peered closer at Jeff, then held out the car keys. "Here. I can do this by myself. Why don't you go wait in the car? You have your iPod, don't you?"

Jeff felt his shirt pocket and a look of relief came over his face. "Yeah, that's a good idea." He grabbed the keys and took off. In the wrong direction.

Mel called after him and when he turned around, she pointed in the direction of the exit doors. "Oh, right," he acknowledged.

JEFF SETTLED himself in the passenger seat with a sigh of relief. He pulled the lever to give himself the maximum leg room, adjusted the seat back so it reclined, inserted his ear buds, and felt some of the tension leave his body. His noise-canceling ear buds were a lifesaver, blocking out the world when it interfered far too heavily.

This is what he should have done instead of going into that stupid store. Why did Mel ask him to come along? She knew he hated places like that.

And, why was she bugging him so much about

college? Didn't she want him to get an education? She had a degree; why shouldn't he? She went away to school, so what did she think was wrong with him doing the same thing? As kids, she had teased him and well, maybe he'd ragged on her too, but they were adults now. Shouldn't she be over that? How did she think scaring him and dredging up old, horrific memories was an okay thing to do?

He put his head back and closed his eyes. Images of high school flooded his mind. That crowded hallway. The grating, metallic slam of locker doors closing. He just knew that kids watched, waiting for just the minute that he would walk by to rattle their lockers, slam them shut with as much force as humanly possible, then scrape the bands of the locks through the holes that never lined up correctly. The next step would be a shoulder smash into the locker to get it to close properly so the lock could be inserted. Then, wait for it, that irritating click as the lock shot home. Then, even the nicest girl would turn around grinning in triumph, knowing that she had done all she could in two minutes to irritate the life out of Jeff.

And this was all before classes even started.

In his last year of high school, or rather the last year before he left, Jeff had found a better system. There were two sets of doors leading into the school. He discovered that if he waited between those doors, even though he would be bugged by students entering the building, and he'd get alternate blasts of cold air from the outside and puffs of over-heated air from the overhead blower and yes, he'd be overwhelmed by the stink of sneakers and boots left on the boot racks, but on the whole, it was better than being in those crowded hallways.

He had no idea why kids had to be so noisy in the morning. They had not even entered one classroom yet, but they were squealing and pushing and yelling and laughing in the hallways. Had they no sense of decorum? Did they not know how much their giggles, and noise, and fast movements got on his nerves? Well, of course they did - that's why they did it. He was convinced that many of those rotters stayed awake nights plotting the new ways that they could get Jeff.

But it was better waiting it out between those doors, because, apart from all that to contend with, there was the buzzer. On television, schools had bells, some of them not bad sounding. Why did *his* school have to choose a buzzer and such a god awful one at that? Someone had even taken the time to pick a pitch that was guaranteed to send shock waves of revulsion through a person's body. But, here, between the double doors, the sound was at least somewhat muted.

The only good thing about that buzzer was that it sent other students out of the hall. Maybe they couldn't stand the sound either and fled when they heard it. That made sense. Whatever the reason, the hall would become quiet, almost peaceful. Oh sure, there were still all those smells that lingered, but at least the bodies were gone.

And, that meant he could get to his locker without worrying about anyone touching him. Some idiot who liked to torture people decided to make lockers that were narrower than even the tiniest girl's shoulders. How did they expect a whole row of students to get things out of their lockers at the same time? It was a physical impossibility unless you were into pushing and shoving.

Ah, but Jeff had found a way to foil this plan. He'd wait until everyone else had left, then go to his locker. He had also discovered that if he lifted the door instead of just yanking it open, it did not squeak nearly as much. And, yes, his can of WD-40 stored on the top shelf helped. With a look to make sure no one was around, he gave a quick squirt to the hinges of his locker. Then, checking again to make sure he was alone, he applied some to the hinges of the lockers on either side of him. Noting that the National Anthem had not begun yet, he continued to oil the four lockers on either side of him. There. That should help. He had no idea why he had never seen any other students doing this. How could they not know that just a few drops of oil like this would eliminate the squeaks that contributed to the mayhem of the hallway? All of their lives would be easier, including his.

THE DOOR behind his head was yanked open and rustling plastic bags dumped onto the floor and seat behind him.

"Geez, Mel," Jeff complained.

"What? You expect me to get all the groceries myself

then stand out here holding them all day? What's your problem?"

"I was half asleep here and you jerked me out of it."

"Let's just get this stuff home."

"Yeah, well, mom's not going to like the way you handle her groceries."

"That's not all she's not going to like," Mel muttered to herself.

CHAPTER 2

Doreen started up once she and Mel were alone in the kitchen with the supper dishes. "What did you do to him?"

"Him who?"

"Don't get sassy with me, young lady. You know exactly what I'm talking about. Jeff was just fine at lunch."

"Lunch? You mean that meal you made just for him at one-thirty in the afternoon?"

"He was fine when he got up, but then you two went off and he came back upset. He hardly said a word at supper and didn't look at anyone. What did you say to upset him?"

"I didn't mean to upset him. I told him a bit about what life would be like away at college and some of the things he'd have to get used to, some of the things that might be tough for him."

"What did you do that for? We have less than a week

left together. I'd like it to be peaceful and calm. Do you want Jeff to go off in a funk? You know how he can get."

"No, I don't want him to be in a funk or depressed, if you want to call it what it is. But don't you think he'll do better if he's prepared, and he knows what to expect? He's never been good with surprises; he does better when he is prepped ahead of time. You remember that from when he was little."

"He's not little now, and I would like to have a pleasant household for this final week that we're all together."

"Mom, you're not being fair to Jeff. We're not sending him off with a fighting chance if we don't first prepare him for what he'll experience there and help him learn to look after himself."

"Kids figure these things out on their own. You did. It's part of growing up."

"When I left home, I'd been helping out around here for years. I knew how to cook, how to shop, and buy groceries, and how to clean up after myself. Jeff has never done any of that - not one of those things. Ever. How do you expect him to suddenly learn all that on top of coping with university classes?"

Mel just shook her head as she hung up the dish towel. "Mom, you just don't get it."

Doreen raised her hands and eyes heavenward. "How many mothers have had to listen to those words?" To Mel, she said, "I won't have you upsetting everyone around here. Leave your brother alone."

Mel left the room, pretending she didn't hear that

last bit. I'll wait until Mom and Dad are asleep, she thought.

∼

As the house settled for the night, Mel made her way to Jeff's lair in the basement. He'd only been up less than ten hours, so she knew he wouldn't be ready for bed yet. But prying his attention away from his computers would be the challenge.

Oh, this was not good. Not even a single light was on, and two of his three monitors were dark. Jeff was hunched over the middle one, mindlessly following a blip around the screen.

"Hey, Jeff. Can I talk to you?"

No response. His noise-canceling headphones blocked out all sound from the world around him, allowing him to immerse himself into an internal life of his choosing.

She knew better than to touch him to get his attention. While he tolerated touch sometimes, startling him with a hand on his arm was not the way to get things off to a calm start especially now. So, she made her way to the ratty recliner in the corner, pulled the lever to bring up the footrest then turned on the reading lamp by her head.

That got his attention. "What did you do that for?"

"I wanted to talk to you. And, I brought us hot chocolate." She pointed to the steaming cup by his right wrist, the one topped with the miniature, floating marshmallows.

"Thanks. Didn't see it there."

"Jeff, Mom's mad at me."

"What's new about that?"

Mel grimaced. "This time she's mad because she thinks I scared you about college."

Jeff half-turned to face her. "You didn't scare me. You just got me to thinking again about stuff I'd rather forget. It doesn't take much to take me back to the hell that was high school."

"I'm sorry it was so tough on you."

"Yeah, well, you don't know the half of it."

"Tell me."

"I don't think I want to go there again."

"Jeff, I'd like to help you do well at college, but I can't help if I don't understand what school was like for you before. All I'm doing now is guessing."

So, Jeff told her about his reminiscence in the car that afternoon, while she was getting groceries, how hard it was just getting ready to enter the classroom. "And then the teachers would start in."

"The teachers? I thought that the work was not the problem, just the other kids."

"No, I could do the work, at least when I felt like it. Have you any idea how stupid some of those assignments were and how mindless?"

"Actually, I do. And sorry to say, but you'll encounter some of that in college classes as well. You just have to suck it up and do it anyway to get through." She flattened her feet on the footrest and pushed down, then relaxed, causing the lounger to gently rock back and forth.

"Ah, Mel?"

"Hmmm?" The motion was soothing.

"Do you want to quit that?"

Eyes closed, "Quit what?"

"With the noise - that squeaking." He rustled around in the myriad piles on his desk. "Never mind, I'll fix it." Jeff found the narrow tin of machine oil he was seeking, squatted down beside the lounge chair, and got to work. "There. Try it again."

Mel returned to her rocking and relaxing.

Jeff wedged himself between the lounger and the day bed and applied some more oil. "There. That's better."

Mel was not sure she could hear the difference, but whatever. "Where were we? Oh, yeah, you were talking about dumb assignments. Like what?"

Back on his own side of the room, Jeff leaned forward with his elbows on his knees. "Take history class. This idiot teacher started talking about things that just didn't happen. He wanted us to pretend what would have happened if different countries became Allies in the Second World War. What is the point of that? It didn't happen." Jeff's voice rose. "History is about facts. They can't be changed. You can't go back and rewrite history a different way. It was not make-believe. There's none of this what-if crap. It either was that way or it wasn't."

"Why do you think he wanted you to talk about that?"

"He was just messing with our minds. And didn't he pick a lousy time to do it? The State tests were coming up. Have you looked at the curriculum and how many standards have to be covered?"

"Actually, I have a degree in Education, so yeah, I have a pretty good idea about the curriculum."

"So why waste our time on fairy tales?" Jeff shook his head. "You might expect that in English class, but not in reality-based subjects. In fiction, things don't have to make sense, but in history you deal with facts."

"Not sure I agree with you, brother. Lots of things that have taken place in history are not logical and don't make sense."

"They made sense at the time, at least to the people who made the events happen. But facts are facts; they happened, and we're not going to change that reality."

"Okay, let's let that one go for now. But do me a favor - don't take any History classes at college. I think they'd drive you nuts."

Jeff drew back his head to regard his sister. "Now, *that* doesn't make sense. I'd have thought that History was one of the more straight-forward subjects to study at university. You memorize a bunch of dates and events and names. That's what it's all about."

"Not exactly. Part of the reason we study history is to figure out why those things happened, the motivations behind the acts and the consequences so that hopefully we don't repeat the same mistakes again."

"We're not getting into human motivations again, are we?"

Mel debated. "No, we won't go there tonight." She grinned. "But, first thing tomorrow morning…."

Jeff regarded the ceiling.

"Just kidding. But I do have a good idea for tomorrow morning."

"Morning? You know I don't do mornings."

"This is for a good cause. I think you and I should get in the car and drive to your new school first thing in the morning. You can sleep all the way there if you want."

"Why would I want to go there tomorrow? School doesn't start until September 5th. That's a week away yet. No one will even be in classes yet."

"That's the point. We could go when it's nice and quiet since most of the students won't have arrived yet. We can check out the campus, find all your classrooms, get your student card set up, go eat at the cafeteria, look at your dorm room and all that stuff."

Jeff looked at Mel as if she had lost her mind. "I've heard stories about cafeteria food. I'm going to be doomed to eat it for the next eight months. Why would I want to start a week early?"

"To get used to the place. To find your way around when it's quiet and peaceful there. To walk through things without the stress of having to get to class on time and with everyone else bustling about."

Jeff shook his head. "I don't think so, Mel. I'm going to be there soon enough. I'd rather relax at home for as long as I can. Besides, I have stuff to do." He pointed at his computer array.

Mel tried another tactic. "Since you've never even seen your dorm room, you have no idea how much you can take or even if there's room for all this, this stuff." She pointed at his computers, monitors and whatevers.

Jeff's eyes widened and he spread his hands protectively toward his equipment. "These are not optional. Where I go, they go, or I don't go." He turned his back on Mel and booted up the left-hand machine.

"That's part of what we'd figure out by going there early to take a look. Right now, you don't know how much desk space you'll have." She thought a minute. "Maybe if we looked, we could see that you'd have enough room if you mounted some of these monitors on the wall. We could go buy the mounting hardware and even put them up before you have to start classes so your place would be ready for you."

She had Jeff's interest, at least for the moment.

"Nah," he shook his head. "It's not worth it. I've got too much to do here to waste a day driving all that way."

Mel let out a breath. She had not thought this would be easy. Better grab him before he became too deeply engrossed in either a programming project or a video game. There'd be no dragging him out of either of those.

"Jeff, since you have a couple of monitors ready, let's try something."

It was not often that Mel expressed interest in his favorite subjects, so Jeff paused to look at her.

"Which subjects do you want to take at school once you get there?"

"You know that computer science is what I'm going in for."

"Yeah, but what exactly within computer science? Have you looked at the course offerings? Now is the time to pick your classes."

"I thought I'd sit in a bunch of them, then pick the ones that seemed interesting and keep going to those."

Mel shook her head. "It doesn't work that way."

"Why not? It makes the most sense."

"Well, it just doesn't. You have to pick your classes ahead of time and those are the ones you'll go to for the first semester, from September to December."

"What if I don't like the class once I get there?"

"Tough. You go anyway, do the work, and finish it. It's just four months.

"It's not really time wasted. You learn something from every class and from every professor - that's part of what university is about. You open your mind to new things. Think of it as building blocks of a foundation."

"I already know things and I know what I want to learn."

"I know you do and that's better than some students who have no idea of what direction they are headed in. But even though computer stuff is what interests you, you will have to take some other classes as well."

"No one told me this before."

Holding her patience, Mel explained, "It's just the way it is. Look, when you're doing your regular computer whatevers," she waved her hand at the nearest screen. "You sometimes wade through stuff you don't like as well to get to what really interests you. College is like that." She paused. "So is much of life, actually.

"Look, why don't we look at your class options right now. Can we use a couple of these monitors?"

"Not this one. I'm doing some work in GIMP that

I'm struggling with. That's why it's black right now. But we can use these two. What do you want me to pull up?"

"On one, bring up a map of the campus so we can see where buildings and classrooms are located. We should try to choose classes that won't have you sprinting halfway across campus to make it to the next class on time."

"Mel, I don't sprint. You know that. I don't like sprinting or running or jogging. I'm not going to have to take up running if I go to college, am I?"

"No. We'll plan your classes so that walking is all that will be required. Deal?" She pointed at the center monitor. "On this one, log into your school's website, then we'll look at your class options." She waited while Jeff typed an overly long password that she would never have remembered unless it was tattooed onto her palm. "Let's go first to the computer science department's webpage."

Jeff navigated there and looked with interest.

"You've never looked at this before?" she asked.

Jeff shook his head as he read about the various areas and degrees possible. "There. That's what I want to take - bioinformatics. Or software engineering with robotics."

"Okay. Now let's see what you need to get into those programs."

Jeff looked at her. "I've already been accepted into this college."

Mel withheld her sigh. This was going to be more difficult than she'd thought, and she wished that she had started earlier in the day. Although Jeff came awake at this time of night, she was near her nodding-off time.

How to explain this? "So, here's the deal. You can choose your major, which in your case is probably computer science. But within that major there are some classes that are required and some that are electives."

"What's the difference?"

"Required classes are ones that you have to take - and pass if you want a degree in that subject. Then besides those required classes, they usually give you a group of other classes to choose from in your field. You'll need a certain number of computer science classes to get your degree. But those aren't the only things you'll need. You will need to take classes in other areas as well."

"I'm going to school to learn more about computer programming. I'm not interested in basket weaving or in character motivation."

"I know, Jeff, but you will have to take a variety of classes to graduate. There will be lots to choose from so I'm sure you can stay away from anything to do with basket weaving."

Ignoring his sister (and the world, she thought), Jeff perused the course titles, clicking on their descriptions.

"I'm done in, Jeff." Jeff shot her an irritated glance as she rummaged through his piles, looking for clean sheet of paper. "Here. Write down the names and numbers of the courses that interest you. We'll look at them in the morning. Remember, a full load is five classes per semester, although you might want to just take three this term as you get used to things. I'm going to bed now." She doubted he noticed when she left the room

~

Mel made two cups of coffee and tiptoed down the stairs, not wanting to awaken Jeff if he was still asleep. At seven in the morning, that was a good bet.

He was poised exactly as she had left him the night before, pasted in front of his computer. Glancing over his shoulder, she saw that he was still on the same website as when she'd left last night. Good. He'd gotten up early to go back at it. She let the aroma of fresh coffee waft under his nose.

Jeff shoved it away with one hand. "Get that away, Mel. Don't tempt me. If I have coffee now, I'll never sleep."

"The effects of one cup of caffeine will have worn off in the next sixteen hours before you go back to bed." She paused. "No, wait. Don't tell me you didn't get to bed last night?"

"What do you expect? You told me to go through these courses to see which interested me."

"It took you eight hours to pour through the computer science possibilities?"

"Of course not. I finished those in a of couple hours. You said I had to take other classes as well, so I'm going through everything. I'll be finished soon. Man, they offer a lot of choice at college. Who'd have thought anyone would study some of this stuff? But you're right. Some of it is interesting and not just programming classes. You could spend a lot of time taking classes. It's going to be tough if you say I can only take five at a time. Maybe they'll make an exception for me. After all, I did grade eleven and twelve subjects pretty much all in one year."

Mel needed more coffee. "Hang on a sec. I need a refill." Again, he hardly noticed her exit.

Back upstairs, Mel shut the basement door softly then leaned against it, the side of her coffee cup resting on her forehead. *What have I done?* She thought back over her instructions to her brother the night before. No, she had not been specific. She assumed that he'd only look at the computer science class possibilities, but she had not explicitly given him that narrow parameter. She had emphasized that he'd need to take other classes in addition to those in computer science. *Dumb, dumb, dumb. She should have known better.* Okay. Deep breath and more coffee. Then she started back down the stairs, apology in hand.

"I'm sorry, Jeff. I didn't mean to waste your time on this." She gestured toward the computer screen.

"Waste my time? This was fascinating, Mel. I had no idea there was so much stuff outside of computer programming that would be interesting."

Mel glanced at the blank paper she had left him the night before - still as pristine as it had been nine hours ago. "Oh, no, Jeff. You didn't think you could remember everything, did you? Why didn't you write down the courses that interested you?"

"I know you're six years older than me, but you are so old school. How would I fit everything on that one little piece of paper? And, what if it got lost?"

Mel looked at the disaster that made up his desktop. "Yes, that could happen."

Jeff opened his third monitor, surprising Mel.

"I thought that one was sacred," she said.

"This is important, too."

Ah, progress, Mel thought.

He opened a complex spreadsheet. Mel leaned forward to try to make sense of what she was seeing. Proximity didn't help. "Explain, please."

Rapidly, Jeff flipped through the pages, things whizzing by at a pace too fast for Mel to make any sense of it. Jeff pointed. "Everything is divided by year, then by terms. You said that a degree usually takes four years. I might need to stretch that a bit to get everything in. Then you said that a semester is four months long and there can be five classes per semester. Since there are twelve months in a year, that means four semesters per year at five classes each, so twenty classes a year, times four years, so I could fit in just eighty classes. That isn't going to work; I need to take more than eighty courses."

Mel closed her eyes. Jeff nudged her.

"Look. Pay attention, Mel." He pointed. "See? I took your advice and wrote everything down. Here's the course number and here's the course name. You'll note that there is a preponderance of higher numbered courses; they seem to be the most interesting. The eight hundred ones are best."

"Oh, Jeff," she moaned.

"I knew you'd be impressed. Glad you suggested that I do this. College is going to be even better than I thought."

"No. No, no, no."

"Yes, it will be. There is some neat stuff you can take here."

"No, you can't take all those classes."

"Well, not at the same time, I get that. See on this spreadsheet? I've got them all listed in the order I want. First, I arranged them from most interested to those that didn't seem quite as good but were still all right. Then I thought that I should mix them up - you know, take some of the very best ones along with some that aren't ideal, just so I don't get stuck with a bunch of possible duds at the end."

Mel sat back and covered her face with her hands. Jeff didn't notice but kept right on pointing out some of what he saw as the best offerings. Mel peeked between fingers at the number of graduate level classes he had entered onto his spreadsheet. "Uh, I'll be right back." She escaped back up the stairs.

DOREEN WAS MIXING batter in the kitchen when Mel entered. "Why were you downstairs bothering Jeff? You know he is always asleep at this time of day." She tsk, tsked as her attention returned to her recipe book.

"Oh, mom, we might need help with this one. Jeff, he's down there picking out which college classes he wants to take."

Doreen regarded her daughter over the top of her glasses. "You say that as if it's a bad thing. I seem to recall you choosing your classes before your started college."

"But it's the ones he's choosing. He's picked graduate level classes, upper year classes when he hasn't even finished his first year."

"He'll get there, dear."

"No, you don't get it. He expects to take those upper year classes *now* and he won't be allowed to. You have to take the lower level classes first, so you have the prerequisites to take those upper year ones later."

"Jeff's smart. Maybe they'll make an exception for him once they see what he can do."

Mel groaned. "It does not work that way. There will be no exceptions." She poured herself another cup of coffee - her third within the last half hour. Her stomach would be angry with her later.

"Not sure I see the problem. You wanted your brother to prepare for school, didn't you? Well, he is."

"But what he's doing is not realistic. He will not be allowed to take the classes he is picking. It's great to see him enthused, but mom, how do I burst his bubble and make him see that he has to take baby steps before he gets to the really good stuff? And, I will admit that some of those first-year classes are not the most interesting. You have to have an introduction to the lingo of that subject and its history before you get to use the information in applications."

"Melanie Nicols, are you telling me that college can be boring? I certainly hope not, but I'm afraid that is what it is sounding like."

"Mom, some of it is boring. Much of it is great, but yeah, some is boring, and you just have to get through it. And, you are required to take subjects in a number of different areas, some far removed from what you thought you were going to take at college."

"Jeff is not going to like that. He hated some subjects in high school and just refused to do the work if he thought it was boring or pointless." Doreen sat down across from her daughter. Mel had their mother's full attention now. "You were away at school yourself through the worst of his high school days." She shook her head. "Those kids. I thought they'd be the death of him."

"He's told me a bit about that."

"They were tough enough, but it wasn't just the kids. The teachers didn't get him either and he didn't get the kids. The teachers didn't understand that Jeff was different, that he was special and that he shouldn't be expected to do the same things they put the other students through."

"Mom..."

"No, I mean it. Your brother was so far above the other students in terms of brain power; he was likely far smarter than many of those teachers as well."

Louder, "Mom!"

"Well, you don't know what it was like!"

"Mom, there are standards that must be met."

"I'm quite sure that your brother was way above any standards that apply to the majority of those youngsters he went to school with."

"I mean State Standards. Each subject has a curriculum that must be followed, goals and outcomes and indicators that must be met before a teacher can give a student credit for completing that class. *How* they deliver the lessons is often up to the teacher, but *what* they teach is out of their control. Then there are the required tests that are given state-wide in each subject. The teachers have to cover the material that will be included on the test. And to cover that material, there are exercises and assignments that have to be done."

"Those hardly applied to your brother."

"But they did, and they do."

"I know that he knew much of that stuff before any teacher discussed it in class."

"That may be so, but each student still has to demonstrate his knowledge of it in the accepted way. There can be some adaptations, but the Standards must still be met."

"I can tell you that Jeff did not like it. He thought many of the assignments were useless and a waste of time. He found more interesting things to do."

"Yeah and that's why it took him almost two extra years to get his high school diploma."

"As I said, he was busy with other things."

Mel reached over and squeezed her mother's hand. "I know, Mom, and I have some idea of just how tough high school was on him. I really, really want this next school experience to be better. And, it can be. The kids will be different and more mature. Plus, Jeff's matured as well now. He won't have to sit in a classroom all day with the same group. And, if he doesn't like an instructor, he only needs to tolerate him or her for four months, then never see that instructor again.

"I really think he will like some of his subjects and the projects he'll be assigned," Mel continued, "especially once he gets to the upper year classes and the projects he'll be assigned. But first he has to slog through the first-year classes and take the classes that are required *before* he's allowed to register in the ones he really wants to take."

"And you don't think they'll make an exception for Jeff, even if we tell them that he is gifted?"

"Mom, university is full of talented and gifted students. They all still have to jump through the same hoops to get their degrees."

"Hmmmph. I don't think much of them if they won't recognize how special my son is."

Mel shook her head. As her mom returned to her mixing bowl, she tried again. "How am I going to get this through to Jeff? He's excited about school now; he stayed up all night researching classes. How do I tell him that he can't take ninety percent of them?"

"You'll find a way, dear, and I expect you to do it without dampening his spirit."

Yeah, right, Mel thought. She refilled her coffee mug with the dregs of the pot and trudged back down the stairs.

SHE STOOD in the doorway watching her brother, one shoulder against the doorway, both hands cupping the cooling mug of caffeine. He was still at it - after what? Nine, ten hours? Oh, to have that kind of enthusiasm and concentration.

At twenty-six, Mel felt old and jaded in comparison. When had she last felt that kind of passion? She remembered. While she didn't feel it right now, she recalled when she got in a classroom and when she surveyed her new group of students, many of whom were autistic, she knew it. She knew the drive that her brother was experiencing right now, the quest, the inner need to know more, to learn, to do the very best that she could.

Yes, she got it. With Mel, it was a drive to learn more so that she could help more, reach more kids, understand what might be going on in their brains and to help them survive, adapt and thrive in their environment. She knew that university classes for her were a means to an end - she would take what knowledge she could glean so that it would help future students.

But with Jeff, it was different. His was a quest for knowledge for knowledge's sake. He wanted to know, not for some personal or specific end goal, but to learn for learning's sake. While she did well at school, she thought that students like Jeff were really what university was all about. Their mother was right. The school should recognize students like Jeff.

But, first, he had to get there. And, he had to get through first year. That was where she came in. With a sigh, she pushed off the doorframe. It creaked.

"How are we doing with this, Jeff?"

"Great, Mel. This is even better than I had hoped. There are some really neat classes here. And, I've been looking up the professors; some are iffy. I'm not sure they should even be there, but who knows who hired them? Some, though, have done neat things and have interesting research projects."

Ah, an opening. "Some of those profs look for students to work with them. Mostly they want graduate students, but you could look at that down the road."

"Down the road? I'm ready now."

"No, actually, you're not."

He ignored her, so she tried again. "Show me what has you so fired up."

"Lots of possibilities but look at this." He pointed at a tab on the third monitor. "They're looking for summer students to work in experimental quantum information processing."

"What's that?"

Jeff launched into an explanation so technical that Mel held up her hands in a time-out position. "Whoa, whoa, Jeff. I don't get a tenth of what you're saying."

"In simple terms, it is based on the premise that information systems depend on the principles of quantum effects physics."

"Riiiight. Jeff, I don't get it, and I don't care to get it. Glad that you like it and understand it, but that's not the point."

Jeff just looked at her.

"Let's look at the qualifications needed to get into this summer project." She scanned for a few seconds. "There. There's a list of the classes you need to have completed. Ideally, they'd like students who have already finished their Bachelor of Computer Science degrees and are enrolled in a Master's program. But at the minimum, you need to have finished these classes." She regarded her brother. "Jeff, you have none of these. Yet. Once you get some of the first- and second-year classes under your belt, you could stand a chance of getting into something like this." Then she noticed part of the page's heading. "This was a summer project. This is the end of August; you've already missed out on this, but you could try again next year, or the year after that."

"But this is what I want to do."

"Hoops, brother, hoops. Much of life is about jumping through the hoops before you get to do what you want to do."

"I'd rather skip some of the boring stuff."

"Who wouldn't? Jeff, there are actually some good reasons why you have to crawl before you can walk."

He wrinkled his brow at her. "What are you talking about. It's been almost two decades since I crawled and learned to walk. I don't exactly remember it, but that's about the timeline mom talks about."

"I mean that first you have to go through the steps, like taking first year classes before you take second, and so on. Mostly, first year classes are the ones numbered in the one hundreds."

"Have you looked at the hundred classes? They're mostly introductory stuff."

"Right!" She was glad he had noted that. "That's where you have to start."

"What if I'm above all that? Is there some kind of test I can take to prove it or talk to someone?"

"Nope. University does not work that way."

"I don't think I'm going to like this."

Silently, Mel agreed. "Let's go back to the computer science department and take a look at their degree requirements to see what you should register in for now."

Jeff navigated them back there. "Some of this doesn't apply to me. They have a lot of other stuff listed here, things that don't even apply to computer studies."

"That's why they call these liberal arts degrees. You come out a more well-rounded person for having had exposure to a number of different disciplines."

Jeff tried to return to the monitor number one that displayed the information on quantum processing.

Mel dragged his attention back to where she pointed. "Here it lists the suggested classes you take in your first year if you are interested in a degree in computer science." Perusing them, she saw that they wouldn't hem him in; if he wanted a different major, they would probably be applicable anyway. She read for a few more seconds. "So, you should take Computer Science 111 for sure, then Computer Science 113. You should take English 101 since that is required for pretty much any degree you'd get. And you'd need a first year Calculus."

"Calculus! No way. I hated that stuff."

"Doesn't matter. You passed grade twelve math, so you should be able to do this. And, see here?" She pointed to the prerequisite chart. "You can't get into most of these upper year Computer Science classes without first passing Calculus."

CHAPTER 3

Jeff surveyed his room. His new room. So, this is what a dorm looked like? *This* was it? He was bumped from behind by his mom carrying a box. Right behind her, his father had both arms full of more cartons. They were helping to move their son into his college dorm room.

Jeff looked around some more. The room held two small single beds with rubber-covered mattresses with yellowish, lumpy-looking pillows on each. In between the heads of the beds were two small three-drawer dressers. Against the wall near the foot of each bed was a desk. Each was about one third the size of just one of the tables Jeff usually used to hold all his computer equipment.

Two beds. That didn't even make sense, but maybe he could use one of the beds for storage. No, a computer or monitor on a mattress just would not work. The mattress would absorb too much of the heat and things would fry.

So, how could this work? If he pushed both desks together then moved the two dressers behind the desk ensemble, there just might be enough room for a minimal amount of his equipment. Then he might have to look into Mel's idea of hanging the monitors on the wall.

Mel. Right now, he wished he'd taken her up on her idea of coming a day early to check out the room. But it was too late now. Hey maybe if he and his dad pushed that one bed right out of the room, they could make more space.

Well, he would just have to make the best of it, even if this was not the most ideal room by far. Jeff began unpacking his computer monitors, the consoles, his speakers, and peripherals. There was buzz around him and some pesky murmurings but they barely registered. He had work to do. His left shoulder jerked hard up and away when someone poked it. He whirled to find his mother standing far too close. He leapt back, knocking over a chair. "Geez, mom. What did you do that for?" He brushes at his shirt with his hands.

"Your mother has been trying to get your attention. You didn't respond when she spoke to you several times," his dad prodded.

Doreen repeated, for the third time, "Jeffy, you need to get settled in. Where do you want your things to go?"

Jeff half-turned to look at his computer gear spread across the two desks. "What do you think I am doing?" He was arranging his things the best way possible in the limited space this place afforded him.

"Where do you want these things?" Doreen gestured to the boxes of clothes stacked on one of the beds.

"Wherever you put them is fine." He returned to the task of sorting out his desk.

"Jeff! These things must be put away. Which clothes do you want in the top drawer?" Doreen could be persistent.

"Mom, I don't care. It doesn't matter."

"Why Jeffrey Nicols! Of course, it matters."

Jeff knew that tone and had learned that when she started like that, she would not be put off. Big breath in. In through the nose, hold it, then out through the mouth. Mel's words rang in his head. She definitely had experience with dealing with their mother when she was in a mood.

Before he had taken more than two deep breaths, his dad stepped in.

"Doreen, you know that you are better at organizing things than either Jeff or me. So you go ahead and put his clothes away in the spots that you think best. He'll find them when he goes looking. Right, Jeff?"

Jeff nodded, too distracted by the need to organize his computer supplies in this cramped space. When he had done the best he could, he pulled the desks out from the wall so one was leaning against the end of one bed. Not ideal, but he could sit on the bed to work. Then he moved to where his mom was working at the dressers, opening drawers, packing in folded clothes, and then moving on to the next drawer. With a grunt, he heaved the empty dresser up onto the bed, across it and off the bottom end. He shoved it between the wall and first desk, effectively multiplying his tabletop space. There was a height differential, but he liked his monitors a bit taller anyway. This might not be so bad after all. He stood back to admire his arrangement. Yes, he could make this work. He retraced his steps toward the second dresser and grunted as he tried to heft it. His mom had packed it full of things and the unit was now too heavy to lift.

Ah, an idea struck. This second bed was the problem. If it was out of the way, then he could shove the dresser into position. Jeff took hold of the mattress and lifted. It wasn't too heavy, just awkward, but someone had positioned rope handles along the long sides just for times like this. Obviously, Jeff was not the first person to want to get rid of the extra bed. As he started out the door with the mattress, his dad called to him.

"Jeff." Louder now, "Jeff, what do you think you are doing?"

Jeff paused, did that breath thing again for patience then stated the obvious. "I am moving this bed out of here."

"Then where is your roommate supposed to sleep?" Doreen asked.

JEFF STOPPED DEAD, the mattress sagging from his hands.

"Bring that thing back in here. Your roommate could arrive any minute and what's he going to think?"

"Roommate?"

"Yes, of course," Doreen replied. "You remember." She waved him back in. "Hurry, before he gets here. He could get the wrong idea and think that he's not wanted here."

"He would get the right idea because he's not." He frowned at his mother. "What's going on? Who said I'm supposed to have a roommate? You know I prefer to be on my own. I don't want anyone messing with my stuff." He swung his arm toward the desktops crowded with computing components.

"Now, Jeff we discussed this." His mom attempted to pat Jeff's arm, but he moved it out of her way. "Remember when we filled out your dorm application? It was a lot cheaper to share a room; the price of a single was exorbitant and besides, this is a nice way to make a new friend."

"I don't need a new friend and I don't want a new friend. Mom, how could you do this? You know how I need my space." He dropped the mattress; it made pacing too difficult. As he strode back and forth, he muttered too low for anyone to decipher.

Hugh turned his back to Jeff and said in a low voice to Doreen, "Maybe we should have listened to Mel. Remember she tried to tell you that this wouldn't work, that you needed to get Jeff a single room? She said to at least prepare him if he was going to have to share. Maybe we should have driven up last week just to look around, too. Our daughter is not always wrong, you know. Sometimes you just get your back up and won't even hear what she has to offer."

"Now, Hugh, don't you start with me. This could be

the best thing that ever happened to our boy. He'll make friends, and fit in and will have a lot of fun this year. You just wait...."

Hugh regarded his wife. Sometimes he wondered what world she lived in. Did she really not know their son and what would make him happy? He shook his head. Derailment time. Before he could interrupt his wife, there was a rap on the door.

CHAPTER 4

They all turned toward the half of the young man's face that was peering around the door. "Um, this is room 305, isn't it? I can't see behind the door to check. This mattress is blocking the way." He walked fully into the two feet of open space he could wedge himself into. "Wow. They really left this place a mess, didn't they? I thought the room would be all ready for us." He glanced some around more. "It's not like there's a lot of furniture for us to arrange though. Won't take but a few minutes, but boy, there's sure not a lot of room in here."

The silence got awkward, but Jeff recovered first. He, after all, had had social skills drummed into him by his sister, and she had revisited the list last night before he left for college. He disengaged himself from between a desk and dresser, leaned over the desk and and stuck out his hand. "Hi, I'm Jeff. Jeff Nicols." The young men shook hands.

"I'm Phil Henderson." He looked at the older couple. "Are these your parents?"

"My mom, Doreen and my dad, Hugh Nicols." They nodded and said their polite hellos.

"My dad's looking for a parking place close by so we can bring up my stuff." Looking around, he added, "I don't think I have as much as you do, though." He took a couple of short steps closer to the desks and regarded Jeff's array of components. "Looks like I know who to come to when my laptop gives me grief." He picked up Jeff's mouse. "Hey, this is some gaming mouse." He lifted it to see how if fit into his palm. "Nice."

He seemed to not notice how Jeff and his parents had all tensed. In their household, no one, but no one touched Jeff's stuff. Jeff reached over and rescued his cherished mouse from Phil's hand. "Thanks. I like it. It's the most responsive I've found yet."

Phil's hand moved over toward Jeff's graphics and drawing tablet. "Cool. I've used a small version of this but never one this good." His grasp was intercepted before he could pick it up. "Sorry, but I don't really like people messing with my stuff." Jeff checked out how Phil was taking this. "No offence, but it's just a quirk of mine. It's even more of a problem when my equipment is all a mess like this. I gotta get it organized." He placed the tablet carefully near the back of his keyboard.

"Hey, man, I didn't mean any offence." Phil retreated until the back of his shins hit the bed and regarded his new roommate from a safe distance.

Jeff noticed the silence. "But when I get everything

all set, I'll show you the software that comes with it and you can have a go at drawing if you'd like."

"Yeah, I'd like that. Thanks."

Before any more gaffs could occur, Hugh stepped in. "Jeff, since all your things are already up here, why don't you go down with Phil and give him and his dad a hand with Phil's boxes?"

Jeff looked at the cables and equipment still to be set up on the desks.

His dad continued. "Don't worry, you'll have plenty of time to straighten all that out later." He moved toward his son to help shoo him out the door. "Go along with Phil. Your mom and I can carry on unpacking your clothes here. And we might even have the furniture in some sort of order before you get back."

"You won't touch my computer stuff, will you?"

Hugh put one hand behind his back and crossed his fingers. "We know better than that, son."

DOREEN AND HUGH watched as the young men left the room. As soon as their footsteps receded down the hallway, they sprang into action. Together, they heaved the mattress from the doorway, back onto the bed. Doreen straightened it, while Hugh wrestled the dresser from behind the desks where Jeff had it tucked. When those items were back in their original positions, he asked, "What now?"

Doreen glanced around. "Well, since I already started putting Jeff's clothes into this dresser, I guess this side of the room will be his." She unzipped the suitcase that held Jeff's shirts, already on hangers. "Here. Hang these on one side of the closet and put his shoes on the floor under them." She dumped out the bag containing Jeff's shoes. "I'll start on the bed. You think about how to handle that mess." She pointed at the equipment sprawled across the two desks.

She unfurled the sheets with a snap, then made the bed with precise box corners. She looked at the provided pillow with disdain and placed it on the top shelf of the closet. From the hamper she brought out Jeff's pillow from home, covered it with the case that matched the sheets, then spread the duvet over everything. She knew that that was all the bed-making she could expect from Jeff, although she doubted that his bed would ever look as well-made as it did at this moment.

Hugh was mumbling to himself. "Hate to do it, but it has to be done. And, best go at it while Jeff was out of the room. Less he can say when he gets back and it's all a done deal." As carefully as he could, he began stacking Jeff's computer equipment, praying that he didn't damage anything. He had to balance things just so to fit it all on the one small desk. Not gonna happen, he thought.

He moved the monitors and gently laid them on the bed. They'd have to solve that problem some other way. With those out of the way and placing the two computer cases on their short sides on the floor under the desk, he could just fit all of Jeff's things onto the one desk. "I know Jeff hates having his machines on the floor. He says he needs ready access, so they need to be within sight on the top of the desk." He shook his head then bent to re-attach the cables he'd had to disconnect. "The odds of me getting this just right are...". The rest of his words were lost to the sound of wood against linoleum as Doreen pushed the now bare second desk back to the wall by the foot of the other bed. Phil's bed.

They heard voices in the hallway and froze. They'd done that a number of times but so far, the steps had not belonged to Jeff and Phil. They had taken Mel's advice and came early in the day, but more and more students seemed to be arriving now.

"What do we do now?"

"How are we going to handle this?"

Doreen pulled from her purse a miniature tape measure. "Quick. I think I hear them." She handed her husband the tape measure. "Pretend you're measuring up the desk. Maybe we can say we're going to go see if we can buy something better that will hold Jeff's things."

Hugh was bent over measuring the desk and the wall space behind it, putting numbers into his phone's note taking app when Phil arrived, followed by a man who was younger than Phil and Doreen by at least a decade.

Doreen pasted on an overly bright smile and turned. She pointed at the bare mattress. "At least you have a place to put your boxes while you get yourself sorted out."

"Thanks," Phil said. He had two boxes piled high in his arms and grimaced as he crouched to put them onto the bed. The top one spilled over and out came balled up socks, underwear, and a t-shirt. "Oops." Phil turned slightly red as he scrambled to get his unmentionables back into the box. Somehow his undergarments seemed to have multiplied in number since he packed them last night, and they didn't want to all return to their box. His dad helped by dumping another carton over top of the spilled clothing.

He dusted off his palms on his pants and held out his hand first to Hugh, and then to Doreen. "Hi. I'm Frank Henderson, Phil's dad. Pleased to meet you folks." Jeff's parents introduced themselves, their eyes shifting nervously to Jeff who stood frozen in the doorway, his arms laden with two bulging, plastic cartons.

Quickly, Hugh returned to his crouched position and explained ostensibly to Frank. "These desks are pretty small to hold all the computer equipment my boy owns. So, we were just measuring up how much room there is here, then we're going to take him shopping to see if we can find something more appropriate for his needs." He peered from behind the desk at his son. "Right, Jeff? Sound okay?" He pointed at the now bare desk near Phil's bed. "If that's Phil's desk and this is yours it looks like you're going to need more room, doesn't it?"

Doreen chimed in. "And remember what Mel said about mounting your monitors on the wall above your desk? That's likely another good idea so we should go check out which kind of mounts will work best."

Jeff still had not spoken. Good thing he had a good grip on Phil's cartons, or they might have crashed to the floor when he saw the way all his cherished peripherals were stacked in that small space. And, his computers were on the floor!

Jeff pushed forward, unceremoniously dumping his burdens onto the foot of Phil's bed. He took three quick strides over to the desk, crouched down and rescued first his largest computer, laying it carefully on the bed, then the second one was gently laid on its back beside its big brother. "Mom! Dad, you know..."

"Yes, we do, son. We know how precious this stuff is to you. That's why now that we see how cramped things are in here, we need to go buy something better. We'll have to decide if you want to leave this desk where it is and build around it, or if we can ask to move it out of here altogether."

"How did you get here?" Frank interrupted.

"In our car."

"Well, if you're planning to buy something as big as a desk, I have my truck here. We could haul it back for you if you'd like." He glanced around the room. "Son, it looks like you could use some things as well. Would you like some shelving above the side and front of your bed? You could hold quite a few books and papers on a twelve-inch shelf. And, some shelves above your desk. I agree with Hugh that there isn't much storage room in here.

"Yeah, I don't know where I'm going to put my Play Station."

Frank looked at Jeff's parents and laughed. "You know, the essentials."

While Hugh and Doreen laughed politely, still on

tender hooks about how Jeff would react, Jeff's head came up. "Play Station?"

"I hope you don't mind. I just couldn't leave it behind. It's how I chill out and I think I'm going to need a lot of chilling out time this year."

"Mind? What games do you have?"

As the young men started in on a discussion about the merits or lack of merits of the most recent games, Hugh held up his hands in the time out position. "Guys, hey guys. You'll have lots of time for this discussion later. Right now, let's get shopping."

The group started down the hall, the younger men lagging behind and continuingtheir debate as if they had not been interrupted.

"Why don't you all go in the Nicols' car and I'll follow behind in the truck." Frank spoke mainly to Doreen and Hugh and the boys appeared engrossed in their gaming talk. As they entered the parking lot, Frank asked Hugh, "Looks like our sons have found a common language. Do you speak gaming?"

"Not me. Too much has changed since my old Pac Man days."

While the men laughed together, Doreen offered up a prayer of thanks that the moving in scene had gone as well as it did. Things could have been very not pretty, but you never really knew with Jeff. As they approached their car, she nudged her husband with her elbow. "See? What did I tell you about Jeff making new friends here?"

∼

"Aren't box stores great?" called out Frank as he led the procession into the building. The doors slid open in front of him. The blast of warm air blew on them in that space between the inner and outer doors. Coming in behind them was an employee leading a cart train, it's front light blinking and revolving and the beep, beep noise blaring to warn anyone in its way. To the side was the rattle and clang of carts as customers attempted to separate one from the other in their parking stalls.

Hugh bumped into his son's back as Jeff froze when he came upon the second set of automatic doors. While the entry way somewhat muted the din from within the store, now the full volume hit the shoppers. Many people reacted to the bombardment with excitement, increasing their shopping pleasure, to others the noise was an assault, filling their senses, leaving no place for the rest of their system to process any incoming stimuli. Unfortunately, Jeff fit into the latter category. While Hugh didn't like it either, at least he was able to block it out for short periods of time - long enough to get in, get what he wanted from the store, then get out. Jeff, however, wasn't blessed with such a filter.

In retrospect, Hugh reasoned that this would not have been the store of his choice to canvass with Jeff. But Frank knew the city better than he, so they had followed his truck right to this place.

He placed his hands firmly on his son's shoulders and pressed down. He kept the pressure on while he said, "Jeff, we won't be here long. We're only going to look for a couple of things. We will go to the furniture aisle that has desks. Then likely right beside there will be the shelving and storage units. After we have those picked out, we'll go to this area." He pointed over his son's shoulder to where televisions of all sizes sat, their varying pictures flickering and changing constantly. At least the sound levels were either muted or so low they couldn't be heard from where they stood. "We'll find the brackets to hang TVs to the walls and buy three of them for your monitors. Got that?" Beneath the pressure of his hands, he could feel Jeff's shoulders lowering - not quite to their normal position, but at least they didn't remain locked in that state of high tension.

Jeff let out the breath he had been holding and sucked in a second one then blew it out in a whoosh. "I'm okay, Dad. It just startled me. I don't know why I wasn't expecting this, but I wasn't. Phil and I were talking about the game *Going Home* and my mind wasn't on anything else." He took a few steps in and spied his mother who was waiting up ahead, her brow creased in worry. "Mom's not going to do one of her marathon shops, is she?"

"No son. Definitely not. Neither you nor I want that. She has to go by herself when she plans to spend that much time in a store." He shoved an oversized cart in front of Jeff. "Here, hang on to this for us, will you?"

Frank and Phil had doubled back. "Hey, thought we lost you. Quite a crowd here, isn't it? These places must make a killing." He pointed back from where they had come. "We found the desks. And, right across the aisle from them are the storage units. They must have known what we were after when they planned this place." With that he strode off, Phil behind his dad, giving a look over his shoulder toward Jeff.

As they passed a display of gallon jugs of engine oil at the end of the first aisle, Hugh quickly plunked three into the cart that Jeff pushed. "Dad, those aren't even all the same type of oil. Are you sure you need these?"

"Just keep pushing. We can check later or put them back. Let's go look at the desks." He had hoped that neither Jeff nor Doreen would question his choice about picking up the oil. Mostly he was looking for something heavy for Jeff to push, knowing that heavy work often had a calming effect on his son.

As with many such stores, the selection wasn't huge. In this case, this was excellent as they didn't want to dawdle over endless choices. The main parameter was size and shape so that it would fit in Jeff's side of the room. Luckily, within the choices was an L-shaped unit with dimensions they could work with. The short side of the L had two layers of closed drawers in a hutch, but the long side would open to the wall. Then the decision was to either install a shelf along that wall at the right height where Jeff's monitors would sit, or to purchase three wall brackets to mount them.

It was Phil who helped with that. He had a friend with mounted monitors. The brackets his buddy used allowed the monitors to be tilted up, down or slanted to either side. That appealed to Jeff, who wanted to look at them immediately.

They retraced their steps to the electronics area where in behind the televisions, mounting hardware selections were displayed. He found exactly what Phil was talking about and added three to his cart.

"Now, back to that last aisle. Phil here needs some shelves."

While Phil ended up with a double layer of shelves that would run along the side and head of his bed, they also found-under the-desk storage for Jeff. The bonus was that each segment was on casters so it could be easily repositioned.

While the men measured to decide on size and numbers, Doreen wandered off. She now returned with hanging cloth dividers for the closet. They could stack their jeans and other clothes in these, sort of like soft-sided, multi-shelf locket units. Jeff was noncommittal, but Phil could see the merit in these. He hated to hang things up anyway.

She also had four small LED desk lamps to show them. "Do you think these would work on your desks and on your dressers as reading lights? Then one person could still be working while the other slept without having the main lights on." These too were added to the cart. To make enough room in the cart for in Jeff's storage units, the oil jugs had to be removed. They had served their purpose anyway.

He walked along side Jeff as they made their way toward the tills. "Think this stuff will work okay, son?"

"Dad, that room is still awfully small."

Hugh nodded. "Yes, it is. That's why you'll need to store your stuff vertically rather than all spread out the way you did at home. Actually, you might find you like this way better. It would be more organized and give you more desk-top room. Okay?"

"That part might be all right. We'll see. But mom never told me I would have a roommate. I've never shared a room with anyone before in my life."

"Phil seems like an all right kid to me."

"Yeah, it's not him personally. It's just, well anyone. I hate having people in my space."

Hugh stopped walking to face his son. "You've been rather spoiled at home. Having just two kids, we let you each have your own bedrooms when you were young. Then, when Mel moved away to college, we let you take over almost the whole basement.

"Remember when you found it hard when Mel first moved away?"

"Yeah," Jeff smiled. As much as she can be a pain and we fought a lot, it felt weird in the house not having her there."

"But you adjusted to it. And, you'll adjust to this as well." He turned away since they had made it to the check-out line, and Hugh reached for his wallet.

When their turn came to check-out, each parent paid for their son's purchases. A starting school present, they said. After opening the back tailgate of his truck, Frank left the younger men to stow away their purchases. Doreen tried not to cringe or interfere as she saw the students loading the truck with the first items that they laid their hands on, rather than making the packing determination by size, shape, and weight. But it all fit. and Frank supplied a red flag for the end of the shelves that hung over the back of the truck bed. Stored under the flip-up seats in the back seat of the truck were tie-down ratchet straps. Phil and Jeff secured the load, then they were ready to pile into their parents' vehicles to get back to the dorm.

Doreen looked at her watch. "Anyone hungry? It's almost supper time." They looked at the pile of merchandise firmly tied into the truck.

"Do you think we should leave this in a parking lot while we go somewhere to eat?" Phil asked. Good question.

"Jeff, why don't you go with the Hendersons and you guys can start unloading things and getting them up to your room. How about Doreen and I scout around for some take-out food to bring back with us."

That was the plan. But as they drove off, Doreen remembered that they had forgotten to ask what kind of food Frank and Phil liked. And, they had neglected to exchange cell phone numbers. "Oh, well. It's unlikely that Phil is as picky an eater as Jeff. Let's just get something we know Jeff will eat." Then, he added, "It might be more quantity than quality they'll be seeking after hefting all that stuff up three flights of stairs."

Then the plan went awry.

CHAPTER 5

"You knew we were lost. You could have asked for directions back to the college when you picked up this food."

"We're not lost. We just got turned around."

"Yes, we sure did. *Before* we stopped for Chinese food. And yes, we've been turned around lots since you got the food thirty-five minutes ago."

"That stuff sure smells good."

"I think the aroma is fading and it's probably getting cold."

"Try Jeff again," Hugh suggested.

Doreen sighed, but once again pulled out her cell. "For a techie boy...," she shook her head.

This was a contentious issue in their family. Although they all had cell phones, both she and Hugh didn't always remember to keep them charged. Hugh solved his problem somewhat by keeping his cell on the car charger whenever he drove. Mel was good about hers and Doreen maybe a bit better than so-so. But Jeff was the problem. He refused to keep his cell on. He said he turned it on whenever he wanted to call someone. Neither Doreen or Hugh had been able to convince their son that he needed to keep it on for *their* sakes, not his. What if they wanted to reach him? He'd look blank at that question. "You know where I am," he told them.

Even Mel tried, although Doreen was not thrilled with her tactic. She told Jeff that when she was away, he was all mom and dad had to rely on in case something happened. They were getting older and with that came ailments and health issues. They might need Jeff's help, so he needed to always be available. "I am," he replied. "I'm right here in the basement. All they need to do is yell down and I'll be there."

"But what if they're out shopping and have a flat?"

"They'd call their automobile club, like they always do."

"Jeff, it could be other stuff."

"I don't like to chit chat. I'm too busy for that sort of stuff; you know that, Mel. People use those cell phones for all kinds of trivial stuff. I'm not like that. I don't feel the need to share with anyone what I had for breakfast, and I do not care to hear what they had to eat or what show they're watching on television."

In the end, Mel was not able to convince her brother about the importance of having his cell phone on. Well, partly; at least he usually carried it in his pocket now. Since his watch's battery wore out, he used his phone to tell him the time and the date.

"No answer," Doreen reported.

"How long have we been gone?"

"It's been forty minutes now since you picked up the food, another twenty while they cooked it, then I'm not sure how long we drove around *lost* before we found that Chinese take-out place. At least a half hour, I'd say. Maybe more."

"So, it's been at least an hour and a half since we left Jeff and the Hendersons in the parking lot. Surely, they're wondering where we are? At least their stomachs should be telling them that it's time to eat."

"One of them will ask about where we are. Frank or Phil will suggest that Jeff call his parents. That will make Jeff turn on his phone."

"If it's charged."

"His charger should be there with that carton of computer cords. Or, he could give Frank one of our numbers and he'll call."

Doreen put her back to the door to turn and look at her husband. "And, what good will that do? Sure, he can call, and we'll have a nice old chat, but we'll still be here with the food and they'll be hungry and waiting for us because we will still be LOST." She lowered her voice. "Or, will you tell Frank you're not sure how to find our way back to the campus?"

"There is another way. If only either of us had a smart phone we could look it up on Google Maps." He drove through the intersection just as the light turned green. He glared at his wife before she could comment. "Why do you have just this little flip phone that won't do anything but act like a phone?"

"For the same reason as you - lazy. Too lazy to be bothered going shopping for one because there are so many choices. And too lazy to learn a piece of new technology."

They grinned at one another. They'd had this discussion before.

"Okay, you win." Hugh pulled into a convenience store parking lot. "Let's go ask someone."

Doreen looked at him in amazement. "Really?" In all the years they'd been married....

OF COURSE, the desk did not come as a desk, but in two cartons. Phil's shelves were more straightforward, so after the men carried everything up to room 305, Phil and his dad began installing those. Frank's tool chest came well-equipped, including his cordless drill.

"Jeff, this won't take long. Phil and I will get these put up while you unpack the pieces from your desk. We'll give you a hand in a bit." He shook his head at the pictorial directions, accompanied by a few words that had a passing acquaintance with English.

Jeff tossed all the cardboard wrappings into the hallway, not noticing that anyone attempting to venture down that hall would need to either move the boxes or tromp them down to get by. Back in the room, he opened each plastic bag, dumping them in a pile in the middle of the floor.

"Hey!" Frank said. "Don't mix those up. Each package is likely labelled, and you'll never know which fastener goes where if they're all jumbled in a pile."

Jeff didn't hear.

Frank shrugged and muttered something about some people's kids and how they didn't have a lick of sense when it came to practical things like building. He returned to getting things set up for his son. At least Phil followed his directions.

Sometime later, the drilling and screwing done, Phil began setting his belongings on the shelves, quite pleased at the additional space he now had. His dad's idea to place cupboard doors over the shelves had seemed excessive at first and more work than he thought they'd be worth, but now he saw the point. He had a lot more privacy without his stuff on display. Not that he had anything that precious or personal, but still, it just seemed better this way.

His dad tapped him on the shoulder. When Phil turned around, Frank pointed at Jeff.

Rather than, as he had feared, having to help this young man step-by-step learn how to follow directions and put together a piece of furniture, Jeff had it. Or, nearly had it. He just had to finish putting the doors on the hutch, then he'd be done. One was up, but Jeff was swinging it this way then that. Unsatisfied, he'd adjust one of the four screws on the hinges to get it to hang straight. Without being told, he seemed to understand the mechanism and the function of each of the screws. Frank was about to offer some advice, but he held his tongue, seeing that Jeff was figuring it out.

Earlier this afternoon, he had kind of wondered

about Jeff. He thought the kid was holding back quite a bit, letting his parents take the lead. Maybe this was his first time away from home and he was nervous or scared. Not that Frank really cared about some strange kid but having a scared roommate might make things hard on his own son. Phil would have enough to do with just taking care of himself. It was actually his first time living away from home as well, but at least he'd been out of school a year and had held down a job. So, life wasn't a total mystery to him the way it would be for some first-year kids.

But maybe he was wrong about Jeff. While he had held back with his parents, when it came to practical things like building something, the kid had really stepped up. He doubted Phil could have put this desk together all on his own; hell, he would have had a tough time doing it alone, particularly in this short amount of time. Even though he might not say a lot, the kid had skills. Maybe he had something to offer Phil.

Phil was basically a good kid, but sometimes he had his head in the clouds. He confused play with work. It had taken a full year of working on him, but Frank was confident that they had him squared away now. He was taking sensible classes at college – the kind that would lead to a solid job, one that would support a family one day. Phil needed to meet friends who were on the same path, not ones with airy fairy ideas in their heads. Jeff had a practical bent, just the sort of influence Phil needed.

But Jeff's parents were another matter. Where were they with that food?

CHAPTER 6

Frank's stomach rumbled again. The second time, the volume increased enough that it disturbed Jeff's concentration. Up until then he had been able to ignore the distractions of Phil's and Frank's shelving projects while focusing on building his desk. Maybe it was the frequency or intensity of Frank's rumblings; maybe it was that Jeff's task was completed, but the other people in the room now had Jeff's full attention.

"Pardon my stomach. It fears that my throat has been cut."

Jeff's expression turned quizzical. "Did you nick your throat with your drill bit? I don't see any blood, but I'm pretty sure my mom packed a first aid kit somewhere here." He looked around at the boxes still at the head of his bed. "Or maybe she put it in one of the dresser drawers. Feel free to take a look."

Frank looked at Phil, who raised his left eyebrow.

"No, that's just an expression. What I was trying to say was I'm hungry."

"Oh. That makes more sense when you say it that way. Mom and Dad said they're bringing food for us." He started organizing some of his electronics into the storage bins beneath the desk.

"Shouldn't they be here by now? Were they going to cook the stuff?"

Jeff looked at him oddly. "No, they said they were bringing us take-out food. They would not have any way of cooking it themselves here. They're a long way away from home and mom's kitchen."

Frank tried again. "What I mean is, I wonder if they ran into trouble. It's been well over an hour since we last saw them."

"Has it? I wasn't paying attention to the time."

"Surely they'd call you if they were delayed or they had a problem."

"Yeah, I think so." He remembered his phone and took it out of his pocket and turned it on. The display showed four missed calls, all from his mom's number. "It looks like she tried to call me."

"Are we in one of those areas that drops calls all the time? You'd think in the middle of a city that wouldn't happen."

"I don't know about that. My phone hasn't been on so I don't know if this area has poor cell coverage." He continued peering at his phone for a few minutes, then put it away.

"Did your parents text you?"

"They don't text."

"What does their message say?"

"I don't know."

This kid was a barrel of information. He tried again. "Do you think you should phone them? Maybe they ran into some kind of difficulty and need our help."

"Hm. Maybe." He clicked on his mom's name in his sparse contacts tab. He let it ring twice, then hung up.

Phil said, "Wow, you have fast phones. Mine would hardly have made the connection and rung once or twice in that time."

"Mine rang twice."

"Was her phone not on?"

"Don't know. She didn't answer. If she'd wanted to talk to me urgently, she would have picked up right away. She hates it when I don't pick up immediately; it seems important to her."

Before Frank could think of a reply, they heard voices in the hallway complaining about the mess of cardboard boxes. As Doreen went on about the mess, Hugh told her, "I have a feeling I know where they came from."

The faint aroma of soy sauce, and garlic and something else delectable preceded them into the room.

"Sorry we're late," began Doreen. "We got lost, then we had to find a parking place, then climb over a mountain of cardboard all over the place out in the hallway there." She jerked her head toward the offending area.

Phil looked at Jeff. "I guess we'd better do something with that."

"On our way in, I saw a dumpster just to the right of the door. You could take it all down there."

"You boys do that while I set out the food we brought. Sorry that it's not as hot as you might like, but we got lost getting back here."

As the young men stood regarding the array of containers Doreen unearthed from the bags, she prodded them. "Get. Move that cardboard out of the hallway before someone breaks their neck on it." She continued arranging the dishes on Jeff's new desk along with the paper plates and plastic cutlery the take-out place had supplied.

AFTER EATING, Phil retrieved a garbage bag from the purchases they had picked up that afternoon and held it out as everyone dumped in their used plates and plastic cutlery. There was but a small number of leftovers. Doreen eyed the mini fridge that was wedged in between the boys' dressers. Crouching, she opened the door. Hmm. Maybe room for a small carton of milk, a few apples and perhaps if she packaged things just right, these leftovers all spooned into one container. She tried, then attempted to shut the door. It sprang open under the pressure of the Styrofoam container. She tried again.

Phil relieved her of the leftovers. He looked at Jeff. "Don't know about you, but Chinese never sticks with me. I can likely eat again in an hour or so."

"Ha," replied Hugh. "Sounds like you have a stomach

like Jeff's." He handed his wife one of the empty serving containers and she portioned the leftovers between the two.

There was an awkward pause. No one was meeting the other's eyes.

Phil broke the silence. He turned to his new roommate. "Looks like we know what we'll be doing this evening."

"We do?" Jeff asked. He eyed the food. "Ah, we'll be eating again."

Everyone laughed. Phil added, "I still have some stuff to put away, but not much. Wanna go for a walk around campus?"

Again, there was a pause.

Hugh nudged his wife. "I think he was referring to he and Jeff going for a walk." He looked to Phil. "Right?"

"Ah, yeah. No offence. I didn't mean to exclude anybody, but I just thought that you guys would be anxious to get back on the road."

His dad helped him out. "I don't have nearly as far to go as you two do, but I should get going, too." He linked his hands together behind him and flexed his back. "This moving business is for the young, eh Hugh?"

"You've got that right." Hugh checked out the place. "Think we did a pretty good job of getting these boys settled in. It certainly looks a lot better than it did when you arrived, doesn't it, Phil?" He hoped that Phil thought the mess was just how the dorm room had been before their arrival and not that Jeff had been trying to get rid of his roommate and his bed.

Doreen glanced around the room. To her, the place

still had a long, long way to go. She fretted that Jeff would not finish organizing this space and forever remain in this half-lived-in state as if he were ready to take flight at any moment. She pointed toward the closet. "Jeff, don't forget to...."

Hugh took her by the arm and tried to steer her toward the door.

Doreen was having none of it. "Hugh, he still needs some help. You know it."

"No, he's just fine. He's on his own now. He might not keep this room up to your standards, but then, who does?" He winked at Frank.

Frank moved toward his son and gave him a big, man hug. Phil tried to step back as soon as he comfortably could, breaking the contact. He held out his hand. "Thanks again for all your help dad, and for the shelves and stuff. It made a big difference your being here. And thanks for driving me."

Jeff echoed the good-bye Frank called to him.

Doreen shook off her husband's hand and strode toward Jeff, teary-eyed and with her arms wide open.

"Doreen," Hugh reminded. "Jeff might not want you to do that."

Good call. Jeff took two steps back until his legs connected with the side of his bed. To ward off his mom, he placed his hands on her shoulders and gave them a squeeze. "Thanks, Mom for putting my stuff in the drawers, and to you and Dad for buying the desk and things. Bye." He removed his hands and, since he could not back up anymore, hastily sat down on the bed.

Then Hugh was there, gently pulling his wife out of the way and holding out his hand to Jeff. "Take care, son. Give us a call to let us know how you're getting on or just to chat."

"Chat?" asked Jeff.

"Well, just give us a call."

"Nightly," added his mother.

"Doreen," chided Hugh.

"Well, weekly, then."

Jeff turned his back and bent to gather some computer cords out of the drawer beneath his desk. The rest watched him. And watched.

Hugh cleared his throat. "Well, I guess we're off then."

Jeff looked up. "I thought we already said good-bye."

Frank laughed. "Not one for protracted good-byes, is he?"

PHIL COULD HEAR his dad and Jeff's parents as they made their way down the hall, exchanging phone numbers and best wishes for their son's education experiences.

Phil watched Jeff, who was partially buried beneath his desk as he strung cords. "You don't need to be embarrassed by your mother."

Jeff's head poked out. "Embarrassed? Not sure how that would feel. Annoying is what I'd say about my mom." He reached behind his computer console. "Well, not all the time, but definitely some of the time."

"Then she's doing her job and you're doing yours.

That's part of what parents are supposed to do - be annoying."

Jeff didn't respond.

Phil tried some more. "I'm not trying to insult your parents. I mean they seem like really nice people and all. I could see at the end there that your mom wanted to get into it, though."

"You got that right."

"She means well, but this is your space." He spread his arms. "Our space."

Jeff continued to string his cables. Finally finished, he stood back to look at his desk.

"Not bad," Phil told him. "I didn't think you'd fit all that stuff onto your side of the room, but you made it work. Gotta tell ya, you had me a bit worried initially about just who I was getting for a roommate. But, you're a pretty organized guy."

Jeff's eyebrows lifted and he grinned. "No one's ever said that about me before. In fact, some who know me would be shocked to hear you say that."

"Well, this is the start of our new lives and all that kind of stuff," Phil said. "Want to take a look around campus?"

AT THE DOOR to the dormitory, Phil asked, "Which way?"

Jeff looked up and down the walkway, then glanced up toward the rooftops, before searching left and right.

"What are you looking for?"

"Trying to get my bearings. It looked different on Google's street view. The angle's not right from this perspective. If I could get higher....". He looked around for something to climb and started toward the dumpster where they'd thrown their packing materials.

"Phil laughed as Jeff looked for a way to climb the dumpster. "Good one. You had me going for a minute." He gestured to the left. "I think I saw a sign saying something about a cafeteria that way. Finding where I'm going to get my food is high on my priority list."

Reluctantly, Jeff abandoned his idea of scaling the dumpster for a better view and continued beside Phil. Soon though, his vision adjusted to the perspective from the ground and he was able to use the information he'd assimilated from looking at aerial views of the campus. When Phil halted at an intersection, Jeff said, "This was to the cafeteria. Or at least to the main one."

"There's more than one?"

"Not really, but there are smaller places where you can get some food. They're more like kiosks scattered throughout the campus and some fast food places."

"Sounds like I'm going to blow through a bundle of money if I have to start eating at fast food joints."

"We'll be getting a food card each month. They punch it each time we eat. There's enough on one card for three meals a day at the cafeteria for a month. But instead of getting your card punched at the cafeteria, you can use it for some of these other places, even to buy an apple or chocolate bar or a bottle of water. But there's a dollar limit per month."

"Man, I'll never keep track of how much I've spent on that stuff."

"Why not?" That didn't make sense to Jeff.

"My brain doesn't do numbers that way. Give me a calculus equation and I'm all over it, but keeping track of simple stuff like a budget? Not me. Dad says that I may be good at learning, but I'm missing the practical gene."

"Maybe I can help with some of that. Numbers seems to stay in my head. I can tell you exactly how much I have in my bank account."

"Thanks. If we're eating together often, that will help."

They headed inside the building identified as the cafeteria. Since it was after supper and not all the students had arrived on campus yet, the massive room was fairly quiet. Off to the left was the sound of crockery and pots rattling in the kitchen. As they entered, there were stacks of trays, then metal rails to set the tray while you chose your food. First, there was the refrigerated section where ready-made salads were stacked in clear, plastic containers. Next was the section for jello and yoghurt and cheese cubes. After that were wrapped sandwiches made from white, whole wheat and some other bread that was dark and had bits in it. The sandwich filling was identified on each wrapping. There seemed to be a reasonable choice. Well, except for the bread with the chunks that would get caught in your teeth.

The hot section was only partially filled. In holes minus the tin containers, the steaming hot water below was visible. The food that was still available was the usual assortment of mashed potatoes, mixed peas, carrots and corn, a vat of gravy and some hamburger patties. Perhaps not the most interesting fare, but filling. According to the menu Mel had shown him online, staples were consistently available, and there were at least two different hot meal choices each day and they rotated weekly. Jeff liked that. While he would not want to be forced to eat the same food day in and day out, there was something reassuring to know that Friday was fish day and Wednesday meant chicken. Nice to have something to count on.

They saw where to pick up your cutlery and where to find the coffee and cold drinks. A moving conveyor near the exit seemed to be the place to set your used tray after the meal.

One side of the cafeteria was all glass, overlooking the main walkways outside. Jeff would make sure to never sit by that window. It was freaky with nothing but a pane of glass separating you from a two story fall onto the asphalt below. But there looked to be hundreds and hundreds of other places to sit. That gave Jeff pause. Mel had suggested that he might want to come to eat early or late to avoid the largest of the cafeteria crowds. She had helped him pick his classes around a schedule that would allow for that.

BACK OUTSIDE, Phil asked, "Which way now?"

"Mel suggested that I should find out where my

classes will be held and walk there today or tomorrow to get an idea where I was going. She said it would be easier before all the students arrived, and everyone was rushing to get to class on time."

"Who's Mel?"

"My sister. She's already finished her degree and has one year of grad school finished."

"Is she here?"

"No, she's back home. She's a teacher and she's teaching kindergarten this year. Said she was tired of school, needed a break and needed to make some money. I think she's going to take the last few classes online, then she can work from home on her thesis."

"So, let's go find your classes." He turned back toward their dorm room.

"They're this way," Jeff said.

"Don't you need to go get your paper or whatever, so you know which classes and their room numbers?"

"No, I already read that. I know them."

"Dude, with a memory like that, this place should be a piece of cake for you." He gestured around the campus.

"I don't know about a piece of cake, but I'm not that big on desserts. But Mel says that the kind of memory I have could help at school if I use it the right way."

CHAPTER 7

"Did you get all the classes you wanted?" asked Phil.

"Not even close."

"Did you apply too late and they were full?"

"No," Jeff said. "They wouldn't let me take most of what I wanted."

"Marks not high enough?"

"No, that's not it. Mel says that colleges are sticky about having to take the introductory classes first. Most of the courses I preferred were graduate level, and I can't take them until I wade through this other stuff first."

"Sucks, eh? I'm just as happy taking first year classes. They should be easier while I get my feet wet."

Jeff glanced around at the ground. It had not rained recently and there were no puddles.

"Doubt you'll get your feet wet."

"You're right. I'll just learn as I go." They walked to

the next building. Jeff seemed to know where he was going. "You have a class in here?"

"Computer Science 110. Room 204."

"You memorized the room already?"

"It was listed when I registered for the class."

This gave Phil pause, then he followed Jeff through the door. "I'm taking Comp Sci 110 as well. Wonder if we're in the same class."

"What's your room number?"

Phil shrugged.

"Your section number?"

"Beats me."

Jeff wondered about that lapse. "You have two days to figure it out." He led them up the ramp to the second floor. "I could help you find out which room your classes are in if you want."

"Sure. I didn't pay any attention before. Maybe the information was there, but I didn't notice." As they rounded the corner and Jeff seemed to know to take the hallway on the right, Phil asked, "How do you know which way to go? Does it tell you that as well?"

"No, it just gives the building name and room number. I looked the rest up online and got a map of the campus. Things look different in the aerial view, but I think I can still find my way."

They peered through the glass window in the door to room 204. It was a small lecture theatre with rows and rows of chairs in a semi-circle around a small, raised stage with a desk and podium. In the ceiling a data projector pointed at the white screen hung on the front wall. Phil tried the door. Unlocked. They entered.

Something about the environment made them speak in hushed tones as you would entering a movie theatre where the show had already begun.

"Are you sure this is the right room?"

"Yes," Jeff said.

"Where are the computers? I thought this would be a big lab with banks of computers for us to work on."

"The computer lab is in the basement. We have lab classes as well, but we come here for lectures."

"Lectures about coding? How does that make sense?"

"It does," Jeff explained. "There's lots to talk about in coding. I think we'll be learning to code by hand with paper and pencil."

"Who would do that when there's a computer handy?"

"*We* will. There's a certain amount of logic and flow to work on with each language."

"Which languages will they teach us?" Phil swept his arm around the room.

"I think the course description talked about C or C+ and Java, at least to start with. Some of the other courses get into things like Python and machine language, but not in these beginner, first year courses." Jeff thought some more. "Actually, the class this term is on C, then the next class in January is about Java."

"I only really know one - Visual Basic."

"Have you never coded before?"

"Played around with it a bit, but not seriously. This stuff will be new to me." They turned to leave. "Might be nice to have a roommate who is good at this and can be my tutor."

"Yes, that would be nice. You're lucky that's the way it turned out."

ON THE WAY to the next classroom, Phil asked, "Will Comp Sci be your major?"

"Probably, but Mel told me to keep an open mind, because I might find something that turned my crank that isn't computer related. Those were her words and I know what she means, but I doubt it."

"I'm thinking that I'll go into Biology. But the tech side interests me as well. That's why I'm taking this Computer Science class. Ever heard of Bioinformatics? There are some neat cross-overs between Biology and computer programming."

He had Jeff's interest now. "Yeah, I looked at that. You can get a Computer Science degree in that. I'm not big on dissecting, so wasn't planning on taking many Biology classes, but yeah, there are some interesting applications. Have you seen what they're doing with orthotics now? It's almost like the bionic man stuff has come true."

Phil agreed. "That's what interests me. Although your sister is right. I hardly know what university has to offer, so I'm not locked into anything right now. I just needed a place to start, you know?"

Jeff nodded. They found his English class next. Then, they found his Philosophy class, Ethics of Technology.

"Man, did you actually choose that? It sounds awful.

Good thing you only have to tolerate it for four months."

"Tolerate it?" Jeff asked. "I think it's an important class. Technology is a big part of our lives and only going to get bigger. We need some guidelines as to the directions we take and the decisions we make in how we use technology, especially in the area of artificial intelligence. This class should help me think about that."

"Maybe, if you put it that way."

As they traveled to the next one, Phil asked, "How did you manage to get your classes in buildings all in a row like this?"

"They might be physically in a row, but this isn't the order they'll happen during the day. It's just more logical to travel to them in this order when we're walking around campus now. It's better than zigzagging back and forth to follow my class schedule." He mulled this over. "But that's what I'll be doing once classes start." He muttered to himself, "This is not very efficient."

He stopped in front of room 314. "Here's where I'll have Calculus."

"Seriously? I'm taking Calculus as well. It's required to get either a degree in Biology or Computer Science. Not sure I'm a fan of Calculus but better take it now while I'm taking easier subjects. Plus, it's a requirement if I want to get into some of the second-year classes."

Jeff took off, this time cutting across to the Biology building.

Outside, Phil noticed the sign. "Hey, I probably have a class in here, too."

Jeff stopped in front of the large lecture theatre on the first floor. There was already a sign on the door saying:

~

Biology 101, Section 2
Dr. K. Strunk

~

"That's it for my classes, except for the Biology lab. It's upstairs." He headed for the sign at the end of the hall with a symbol of a staircase going up.

"I wonder if I'm in that class, too."

"When I enrolled, I think the class limit was two hundred and fifty students. It would depend on which section you signed up for. Or, maybe it's the same room, used at different times for different sections. Strunk is my instructor, though. Who is yours?"

"I have no idea. I never noticed when I registered. I don't know any of them anyway, so the names would mean nothing to me."

~

They smelled the lab before they actually saw it. The door was open, the light on and they could hear drawers rattling. They poked their heads in the doorway, feeling a bit like small boys about to be caught doing something naughty.

"Why are you standing there? Come on in. Aren't you curious?"

Slightly embarrassed, the young men entered the room. Jeff hesitated due to the smell. He sniffed the air.

"Ah, the smell of formaldehyde. You get used to it, but it's a bit off-putting at first, isn't it?" the woman asked.

"A bit?" Jeff found it overwhelming. "I don't think I'll be coming in here."

"Oh, yes you will be if you're taking Biology 101. Are you?"

"That was the plan," said Jeff, "but I've changed my mind now. What is this place?"

"This is the lab. You'll spend three hours a week in the lecture theatre, then another four hours per week in here. At least."

"Nope, I don't think so."

She opened a top cupboard and pulled a cardboard carton from a shelf. Digging in, she handed something to Jeff, and then to Phil. "Put these on." When they hesitated, she showed them how to don the mask. "It's not perfect, but it helps a bit. And, you might try breathing through your mouth."

Jeff did, but still found it barely tolerable. "I'm not going to be able to think in here."

"When you were a kid, did your mother ever rub Vicks on your chest when you had a cold?"

Jeff and Phil both guys nodded.

She pulled out another case that held small disks, about an inch around and half an inch deep. She tossed one to each guy. "Open it and take a smell."

When they complied, she watched their faces. "Remind you of childhood?" She took a third one for herself, opened it, dipped in a finger and rubbed a small portion on the skin between her upper lip and nose. "Try it."

Phil did, then grinned. "Hey, I can breathe again."

Reluctantly, Jeff opened his container and brought it to his nose for a smell. It really did remind him of being sick as a kid and having this aroma in the air as his mom fussed over him. He took a tiny amount and rubbed it beneath his nose, waiting for the burning sensation he remembered on the skin of his chest. It didn't come. He took in a tentative breath. Still not good, but better. He rubbed a bigger chunk above his lip, then sniffed. Now two competing scents assaulted his olfactory sense - that underlying chemically smell of formaldehyde plus the camphor under his nose. He took in another big whiff. Actually, the camphor was strongest, attempting to drown out the other, nastier smell.

"I'm Agnes Dour. I'm the lab instructor. You'll be seeing a lot of me."

Phil introduced himself and Jeff.

"How does this work?" asked Jeff. When I signed up for Biology 101, I had to pick a lab section to go with it, but there was no time associated with the lab."

"That's the nice thing about labs. You come and go when you want. Generally, there's about four hours of work to do each week, but you choose when you put in the time. Some people spend a bit of time here each day until it's done; others spend an evening or two. It's up to you, depending on when you can fit it in with your other classes."

The guys thought this sounded good.

"But, let me warn you. Some people put it off, thinking they have assignments due for other classes and forget about the lab. Then suddenly they have three weeks' worth of lab work to get done in a week before midterms. Don't be that guy."

Now that the smell was not so overpowering, Jeff could take in his environment. He walked around the room, inspecting objects. On a shelf were glass jars of preserved baby animal specimens, some in various stages of development. Phil followed his gaze. "Sick," he said. Jeff didn't comment. On the wall was a three-dimensional model of a dissected frog, its skin held open with pins, so its organs were visible. Other pins were stuck in each body part and attached to strings that led to labels. Jeff took it all in. This was the kind of dissecting that interested him.

"Will we be doing some of this?" he asked the lab instructor.

"Yes, frog dissection is part of the course, but you begin with smaller animals such as worms and mollusks," said Agnes. She pointed to more models mounted on the wall.

Jeff wandered to the computer banks that filled the center of the room. "What are these for?"

"This lab involves self-directed study. The lessons

are all online. You pick the lab you need to work on, listen to the lecture, watch the demos then get your materials to do the hands-on part. Some lessons have no activities just an online quiz that you'll do after studying the lesson. Some assignments you'll hand in online; the rest you give to me for marking."

"So, I get to pick the lesson I want to learn?"

"Not quite. I didn't explain that well. The lessons are sequential so no, you cannot jump around. The computer won't let you do lesson four until you've handed in the work for lesson three and received a passing grade on it. When I said you pick the lab you want, I meant pick the next one you should be working on. Since you go at your own pace and come when you want to, everyone will be on different lessons during each section of the course. There is a deadline to have lessons completed before the mid-term exams and lesson fifteen must be completed before final exam time in December."

"Can I get started now?" This was more interesting than Jeff had anticipated. Maybe Mel was right when she said that you never know what will perk your interest.

Delighted to have such a keen student, Agnes readily agreed. "First I need to set you up. What's your student number?"

Jeff rattled it off.

"Good. You're already in the system." She typed for a few minutes on her computer. "Okay, log in with your student number, then you need to create a username and password."

Jeff was ahead of her and was already going through the first lesson's video.

"Do you want to get started too?" Agnes asked Phil.

"Nah. Well, yes, but I don't know my student number." He wandered around some more and then began to get restless. He checked his watch. "You gonna be much longer, Jeff?"

Jeff looked at the progress indicator on the bottom of the screen. "About 190 more minutes to go." He clicked on the next presentation video.

"Well, if you're planning to finish that tonight, I think I'll head back to the room. Kinda tired after moving in, and I still have some things to unpack." He waited to see if Jeff would shut down and join him.

"Okay. See you later."

Phil shrugged at Agnes and gave a half-wave as he left.

CHAPTER 8

Jeff became a regular in the Biology lab. Mel was so right about never knowing which class would end up interesting you. He ploughed through the lab lessons. After listening to the lectures, watching the videos, and learning just why he needed to do the dissection, he didn't hate that part as much as he had thought he would. In fact, he looked forward to the challenge of identifying organs and body systems while performing such delicate operations. It was sort of like building circuit boards, requiring patience and precision.

Although Jeff never got to the point of enjoying or ignoring the smells in the lab, using Agnes' trick of the mask and camphor ointment, he was able to allow the scents to fade enough into the background to allow himself to concentrate on other things. It helped that he brought along his noise cancelling headphones; the more extraneous sights and sounds he could mask, the easier it was to concentrate on what he wanted to do.

While most of the computers were side by side at long tables, a couple sat off by themselves in separate cubicles. One of those Jeff claimed as his own.

Once when he arrived, that computer station was in use by another student. Jeff donned his mask, applied the camphor under his nose and then paced back and forth for a while, staring over the shoulder of the usurping student, waiting for him to leave. At one point the student asked Jeff, "Do you mind?"

"Yes, I do. That's my computer you're using."

The student cast his gaze over the mostly empty room with over a dozen vacant computers. He pointed toward those rows and twisted his mouth to the side. "Use one of those."

Agnes came over and tried engaging Jeff in a discussion about the mollusk he had been working on the day before. She led him to her computer where she had a clip that she wanted to show him about a strange subset adaptation to that genus. Jeff was edgy and kept glancing over toward "his" computer station. Perhaps unnerved by Jeff's stare, the offending student only worked a few minutes longer before packing up and leaving with a sidelong glance at Jeff. As soon as he departed, Jeff took his proper place and got to work.

THE NEXT DAY, there was only Jeff and Agnes in the lab. She took the opportunity to have a chat. If her suspicions were correct, there was a problem.

"So, how are you doing with this class, Jeff?"

"Great. It's way more interesting than I had thought it would be. And, I listened to your warning that first day and I'm not slacking off with lab. See?" He pointed at his screen. "I'm already on lesson nine, and it's not even due until November 18th."

"That's right. It's not due until after the midterm." She pulled up a chair to sit beside him. "Can I show you something?"

Jeff shoved back so she could use his keyboard.

"Have you looked at this chart before?"

Jeff shook his head.

"Well, it's there to guide you through this course. See here?" She pointed. "This shows you how the lab relates to the lectures. By today's date, you should be on class lecture number eight and the corresponding lab is number three."

"Nice that I'm ahead, isn't it?"

"Maybe. I thought I noticed you in here once or twice during the time when your lecture was held."

"Yes."

"Hmm. Do you think that's wise?"

"I'm getting work done."

Agnes tried from a different approach. "Have you been keeping up with the readings?"

"Yes. Definitely, and I'm ahead."

"Show me what you've been reading."

Jeff pulled his lab book from his backpack. "This and the stuff on the computer."

Agnes rolled her chair to her own desk, picked up a book and wheeled back. "Have you read this?"

Jeff eyed the book in her hand. "I think I have a copy of that but no, I have not read it."

"This is the required text for Biology 101. The exams are based part on this text and part on the lectures. I'm worried that you haven't been attending some of the lectures."

"No, I haven't. Well, not many. I did at the beginning, but these labs were more interesting. I'm more of a hands-on guy and the lectures were too much history and background. I'd rather get right to it."

"Me too. I get that." She directed his attention back to his computer monitor. "Would you like to take more Biology classes in future?"

"Definitely."

"Well, in order to take more - and by more, I mean the really interesting ones, you first have to pass this class."

"I'm doing well. You've seen my lab marks; they're excellent."

Agnes nodded. "They are, but look here." She pointed to a line on the monitor. "This is the breakdown of how you get your marks for Biology 101. Thirty percent of your final grade comes from your lab marks. You are doing very well there. But, seventy percent of your grade is derived from your Biology midterm and final exam - thirty percent on the November 3rd midterm and your December final counts for forty percent."

Jeff was quiet, the implications registering. "So even though I spend all this time here in the lab and get great lab marks, that might not be enough?"

"There is no might be about it. You could have perfect marks on every lab, but if you don't attend the lectures and read the textbook, you won't have the knowledge to be able to pass your midterm and final, and you won't get credit for this class. And, that would mean that you can't take any of the upper level Biology classes, the ones I think you would really enjoy."

Jeff's shoulders sagged. "So, that's it? I've flunked."

Agnes patted his shoulder, removing her hand quickly when Jeff flinched. "Definitely it is not too late. It would be too late if you don't make some changes, but you still have time. Your midterm is still three weeks off." Again, she pointed to the screen. "Look here. This shows you the readings from your textbook that you should be doing each week. You are three weeks behind, but you can catch up on that."

Jeff looked skeptical. The textbook looked boring.

"It's not boring. The labs are meant to supplement the lectures and the text. They really do go hand in hand. I can see why you might not have liked the introductory lecture or two; those cover background and terminology and are the driest part of the course. But it gets better, trust me. And, since you are so involved in the labs, you'll see the point of the lectures and how they elaborate on what you're learning here in this room."

"So, I can still make it?"

"For sure. You know, it's usually the other way around. Students attend the lectures but neglect the labs. They get so far behind that they have trouble making up the lab time. And, no matter how well they do on their midterm and final exams, they can't get credit for this course without a passing mark for the lab portion. So, you'll be okay."

Jeff had perked up a bit.

"But no more skipping lectures," she admonished.

Jeff packed up his books and left without signing out of the program or even shutting down the computer. He *never* before neglected security.

BACK IN HIS ROOM, he removed his jacket and shoes. First, he sat on the side of his bed, and then lay down with his arms behind his head. This was what Mel had warned him about, getting so caught up in one subject or one part of it that he neglected the other work he needed to be doing.

He got what he had done wrong in Biology. Sheesh. Just when he was really getting into this university thing. What a loser. He couldn't even manage one class correctly.

A nasty thought entered his head. Biology was just one of his courses. What if he had made the same mistake in other classes? Sure, he hadn't made it to some lectures, particularly the ones that started so early in the morning. Again, he should have listened to Mel when she suggested he pick classes that began later in the day. He'd thought that if a lecture only lasted for an hour, he could get up and go to it, even if he was tired. What was one measly hour? But yeah, it was harder than he had thought it would be.

Jeff glanced over at his backpack resting on his desk. He should really boot up the computer, take a look at each class's syllabus and check that he was on top of the workload for each class.

Who was he kidding? He knew that he likely wasn't keeping up and really was far behind. He'd only been here three weeks, so how could he have screwed up so badly already? Maybe he was not cut out for college. Maybe those kids in high school were right when they'd hold their thumb and index finger to their head, look at him and yell, "loser". He knew they were right then. He should have listened and not tried this school business at all.

That was his last thought as he drifted off the sleep.

THE DOOR SLAMMED behind Phil as he entered their room. "Hey. Ready for some lunch? I'm starving." He noticed Jeff's bleary expression. "Sorry, man. Didn't know you were sleeping. It's almost noon. Wanna go grab some food?"

"Not hungry."

Phil looked at his roommate more closely. "Let's open the curtains and let in a little light."

Jeff blinked at the sudden onslaught of sun. He roused himself enough to bunch a pillow behind his head.

"You look like someone stole your puppy. What's up?"

Jeff shook his head.

"Well, let's go eat." When Jeff still didn't move, Phil said, "Move it, man. We just have time to eat before Calculus class. We're going to the cafeteria *now*." He used his foot to nudge Jeff's leg. "Come on."

Reluctantly, Jeff moved to sit on the edge of his bed, head down and hands dangling between his knees.

Phil kicked Jeff's shoes over toward him. "Let's go, man." As Jeff slowly picked up one shoe, Phil asked, "Where are your books?"

"Somewhere over there." Jeff nodded vaguely in the direction of his computer hutch.

Phil snagged Jeff's Calculus text and the notebook Jeff usually carried and threw them on the bed by the lethargic man.

OUT THE DOOR, Jeff trudged along, shoulders slumped, eyes following the ground in front of his footsteps. As they neared the cafeteria, the din could be heard, even outside. The young men surveyed the crowd of students waiting their turn to join the food line. "It's not too bad today," Phil observed.

Jeff's eyebrows rose then his eyes narrowed to slits. His shoulders and his hands clenched. His breath came quicker. He had never been to the cafeteria when it was crowded. Following his sister's advice, he came to eat before or after the bulk of the students ate. Earlier worked better, but he was often still in the lab. It was quieter if he came later, but sometimes the food options were pretty picked over and they were out of some of the entree options. Coming late also meant that he had to skip Calculus, but at least he could eat in peace. But this, this line-up and the incessant buzz of conversation was an unwelcome experience for him. And, on today of all days. He should never have gotten out of bed.

Phil kept up his end of the conversation as they waited, too wrapped up in his own concerns to pay much attention to the tension radiating from his roommate. "Man, I am so lost in Calculus. Can you give me a hand?" Jeff's lack of response didn't register. "I know you've skipped the last couple classes, but you seem to get this stuff. Maybe we can find enough room at a table to get out our books while we eat. I'd really appreciate some help with this before we get to class, and the prof piles new crap on us. Okay?" this time he waited for Jeff's agreement. "Jeff?"

"Yeah, sure, okay." The line shuffled forward. By now they were in the entryway, the din washing over Jeff. Now he was immersed not only in the hundreds of conversations flowing every which way, but also in the clatter of the plastic trays, the banging of the tin serving dishes, the scraping of the cutlery, and then the conflicting smells of the food and of humanity. Across the way, a crash created a lull in the conversations as someone dropped their tray of food. Then, the voices filled in the vacuum once again. There was an aroma that his mom hated – sort of like some of those times when Mel cooked something but forgot it on the stove, and let it burn. Overlaying that was the smell you got driving by some fast food places. Old grease layered on flattened burgers that had sat under heat lamps too long.

It became hard to pick out individual faces; they kept moving, swimming in front of his vision. Jeff shuffled his feet on automatic, following Phil as he, in turn, followed the person in front of him. With his eyes on Phil's shoulder, he didn't have to think, just copy. As Phil reached for a tray, so did Jeff. When Phil's hand opened the cooler for a tossed salad, Jeff's followed suit. The same cartons of white milk found their way to both of their trays. When they passed by the entree, Phil chose the hot hamburger. The server looked questioningly at Jeff. Phil noticed the pause, glanced at Jeff who was staring over the server's shoulder. He told her, "He'll have the same as me." He took the offered plate and set it on Jeff's tray, and then they shuffled their way to the check-out counter. Phil had his punch card out and ready but had to prompt Jeff to dig his out of his wallet. "Is your head already in Calculus?" he asked.

Jeff didn't reply. He was still in follow mode, which took no thought on his part. Too much of his mind was filled with keeping the bombarding sensations at bay. He needed to just keep his eyes on Phil's shoulders and move his feet. And breathe. That's what Mel would tell him. Breathe. And, none of that shallow crap, filling only the top part of his lungs. There. It helped a bit to hear her nagging voice in his head. He could picture her sitting in his recliner, doing her coaching thing, making him practice. Big breath in through your nose, hold it while you count to three, then out through your mouth.

Again. Again. And, again. Jeff could feel just a bit of the paralyzing tension start to release. Breathe. In through the nose and out through the mouth.

He froze, noticing where Phil led them. Directly in front of them was the expansive plate glass window looking down on the concrete walkways below. That hard, solid concrete, dusty with millions of footprints, imprints of worms squished under the feet of those millions of unseeing students, with only a sheet of glass separating anyone in this room from certain death if they fell through that window.

A nudge from behind sent Jeff forward two steps - forward toward that clear, fragile barrier of a window. He glanced behind, but the tray that had shoved him was long gone, along with its owner.

Phil took a seat at the end of table closest to the window. It was not like there was a lot of choice; these seemed to be the only two places in the entire room where they could sit together. He glanced over his shoulder at Jeff. "Coming?"

Jeff shuffled closer, rounded the table, and pulled out a chair. Behind him, he sensed that window. Turning around, he judged the distance between chair and window to be about six feet. That should be enough room to leap out of the way if anything happened. And, he was at the end near a blank, beige-painted concrete wall. Walls were solid things that would not allow you to be flung to your death twenty feet below.

Phil spread his Calculus text on the table, open to page forty-two. Then he took out his notebook and a pad of paper. "Here's what I don't get." As he tried to explain the steps that didn't make sense to him, Jeff stared at the blank wall to his left, about twenty feet away. "Jeff? Jeff, can you see where I'm going wrong? Are you listening to me?"

"Yeah, I hear you." Jeff pictured his hands grabbing the sides of his brain from the side and swinging his focus back to where Jeff pointed. That was another trick his sister had taught him. Any kind of visualizing seemed to help. Or, at least it gave him something else to think about. That reminded him of what else Mel said. Breathe when you start to feel overwhelmed. Once you have control of your breathing, turn your mind to something that interests you, something that challenges you. Well, Calculus should fit that bill.

He turned his attention to Phil's problem. Jeff had the right instincts and sense of logic; Phil brought the lessons he had picked up from the lectures and reading the text. Between the two of them, they figured it out. As they focused on the theorem, their food cooled on their plates.

Satisfied, Phil picked up his fork and began shoveling in the food. "We don't have a lot of time before class starts. We'll have to move it."

Jeff glanced at the congealing mass of gravy on his plate. He hated it when one food bled into the other; better that they didn't even touch. But this gravy took over everything on the plate. He used his knife to lift the tip of his hot hamburger sandwich. Sopping. The bread was a soggy mess. He could just imagine how that would feel in his mouth - all gooey and greasy and in a lump that would be impossible to swallow. He put down his knife, shoved the plate away and reached for the plastic container that held his tossed salad, all neatly contained and crisp. Sure, there were carrots and tomatoes mixed in with the lettuce, but all the pieces were readily discernible, not overtaking each other. He started in.

"You didn't get any dressing. Here, I didn't use all of mine. Help yourself," Phil offered.

"No thanks. I like it plain." Why muck up a good thing with something that might make it all run together? His stomach rumbled. Glancing over his shoulder to ensure that he remained a reasonable distance from that window, he picked at his salad, eating first all the red bits, then the green.

By now many of the students had vacated the cafeteria, making the place more tolerable. Less bodies, less noise, and less pressure. He could still feel the window at his back, but without the crowds, there was fewer opportunities to get pushed out through the window.

"We gotta get a move on or we're going to be late. The prof scowls at anyone who interrupts his lecture. I think he knows my name. I don't need him to have any bad impressions of me when he marks my midterm next month. I'm going to need all the brownie points I can get." He tapped his notebook. "But you've just given me a leg up. Thanks, man."

Jeff's grip on his books lessened the farther they got from the window. Outside, he drew in a deep breath, but glanced up at the window behind him. It didn't look as threatening from this perspective, but then, he was already safely on the ground. Why didn't they at least have a bar across the lower part of the window or some kind of fence, a barrier to catch anyone who was about to fall through that window? You wouldn't think it met code the way it was. He noticed two girls leaning against the inside of the window, chatting, and watching the students below. How could they put themselves in such danger?

In a few minutes, he and Phil settled themselves into seats near the back of the classroom. The prof finished arranging his books on the podium and turned to his students. "Ah, Mr. Nicols. So nice of you to join us." He wrote on the board:

$$\lim_{x \to 1} [(1/(x-1)) - (1/\ln(x))]$$

"Perhaps you would be so good as to come up here and show us how to do this one." He held out the chalk to Jeff.

FINISHED, Jeff handed the chalk back to the prof, wiped his hands on his jeans and returned to his seat.

"Well, Mr. Nicols. It seems that even if you have not been gracing us with your presence here in class, you have been keeping up with your Calculus studying."

As Jeff began to deny this, Phil's foot connected with Jeff's shin. Phil interrupted. "I was having some trouble with one of the equations from last class. Jeff and I were going over it at lunch. It's the fifth one on page forty-two. Can I ask you about it, or should I wait for the seminar?"

Successfully off track, Jeff's mathematical skills were forgotten.

PHIL GLANCED at Jeff throughout the class. Jeff seemed to be in his own world. Luckily, the instructor did not call on him again. Jeff's gaze remained fixed on the blackboard, although Phil was unsure if his buddy took in anything he was seeing. He had to nudge Jeff when class was over. The rustling of papers being put away, chairs creaking, shuffling feet or conversations didn't seem to signal to Jeff that it was time to leave the room. He caught the prof eyeing his friend and knew he needed to get him out of there. "Move, it bud. Time to go." At least Jeff didn't have to pack up his things; neither his text nor notebook had been opened during the entire class.

ONCE OUTSIDE, Jeff started a brisk pace back toward their dorm.

"Hey, wait up," yelled Phil. "Isn't your English class the other way?"

Jeff gave no indication that he had heard. He plowed through the throngs of students heading in the opposite direction, for once heedless of taking care not to have his arms brushed by anyone. Head down, scowling face, intent on his goal, the sea of students parted in front of him.

Phil shrugged and turned back toward the Bio lab. He was behind and needed to spend time getting caught up.

BACK IN HIS ROOM, Jeff threw his books on his desk, then himself on his bed. With his left arm sheltering his eyes, he tried to nap - his usual refuge when the world pressed down too heavily.

Didn't work. Much as he sought the relief of sleep, it would not come to help him this time. It was easier at home, in his basement, with all his familiar things arranged in just the right way that he liked them. He was used to the click of the furnace when it came on, the swishy tread of his mom's worn slippers as she messed around in the kitchen, even the sonorous snores from his dad as he "rested his eyes" in his recliner in front of the television.

Mel used to tell him, "go to your happy place" when he was really upset. Well, after he'd done the breathing bit, he tried to take stock of his body. No, he was not clenching his teeth. No, his shoulders were not bunched up toward his ears. No, his fists were not clenched. Okay, so that meant that he wasn't tense. Sometimes tension prevented him from drifting off to the oblivious relief of sleep.

Still, it wouldn't hurt to do the relaxation exercises. Starting with his toes, he scrunched them up in his shoes. This really was harder with his sneakers on, he thought. Next, he pointed his toes up toward his knees, held that pose for five seconds, then released it. Slowly he contracted then relaxed each muscle group all the way up to his face. Hmph. Sleep still didn't come. And, he was starting to get tense from the frustration of not drifting off. This was not working.

Other than sleep, his other fail-proof method of shutting off the world was with his computer. Jeff felt its lure, and he settled into the chair as the familiar opening logo appeared on the monitor.

Although gaming soothed him, this time it didn't quite as much as usual. He was unable to totally lose himself in the world of pixels and action and moves; something kept niggling at the back of his mind. Muting the game, and then minimizing it, he opened his browser, pointed it at the left-hand monitor and opened his email program. Message after message scrolled by. His elaborate spam filter weeded out most of the junk. Usually. But his inbox seemed far too full. Better investigate what was wrong with his filter.

Mel! She was spamming him. Checking the dates, he saw that she had started about three weeks ago, on the day that he'd moved here to school. Initially, she sent a message a couple of times that first week, then daily, then this week there were several each day. Geez. What was with her? She knew how much he hated that. Don't send a message unless you had something to say. He would never understand those people who used Facebook like a diary, posting inane comments about what they had for breakfast or taking pictures of everything that floated past their eyes. Even worse were those pictures people took of themselves. Talk about lousy theory of mind - what on earth would make people think that others wanted to look at their mugs or see the world through *their* eyes. They had eyes and experiences of their own.

CHAPTER 9

While most of his class time was spent in the Biology lab, he had made it to a few of his Philosophy classes. Mel had helped him choose which one since he was only required to take one class from the Humanities section, and she thought this was the one he might object to the least. Luckily, there were a few choices and even one that fit with his Computer Science class. It was called The Ethics of Technology.

At first Jeff thought it would be one of the boring things Mel said you just had to suck it up and get through it. But that first class was not so bad. The prof lead with a discussion on 3-D printing and some of the ethical considerations involved. While most people could agree that it was not ethical to clone a person, what about creating body parts? He had asked if this offended the religious beliefs of anyone in the room. No hands went up, although some students looked uncomfortable. Then they watched video clips of some of the amazing ways a 3-D printer was helping people with disabilities. There was this girl born with some syndrome that seriously shortened some of her fingers. But she really wanted to play the guitar. So, a local university created thumb extensions for her, using their 3-D printer. Cool.

Then they talked about orthotics, and hands, arms and legs supplied to people who had lost these body parts. Was that playing God, trying to replicate a part of the human body? Or, was that just people supplementing what we had so that we could better adapt to our environment? Was putting on a jacket or a pair of shoes really a complaint about the way our bodies came naturally? A criticism? Do we have the right to alter or enhance our bodies?

Yeah, that was an all right class and it wasn't a waste to think about these things. Too bad he had not had the time to do the assigned readings; there might have been some interesting stuff in those articles.

Good time to check it out. Jeff pulled up the class site, the one that listed all the required and supplemental readings. Nice. Things were organized by day and by week, showing what he needed to do each day to keep on top of assignments.

Unbelievable! The amount of work the prof expected his students to do. And, that was just for the first week. According to the dates, this was the end of the third week. Crap. He couldn't have done all of this even if this was his only class.

It was too much. This sheer volume of work killed his interest in the class. Instructors needed to be reasonable and understand that students were juggling multiple courses at once.

First, he'd clean up his email inbox, ridding it of all of Mel's spam.

WHAT WAS UP WITH MEL? She usually was not like this.

He scrolled through the subject headings in his inbox. The last four messages from Mel repeated the same heading - "Call home!". Maybe her internet service provider had a glitch and was resending the same message over and over. If so, he should let Mel know. This could annoy people she was trying to contact.

He clicked on the first of the repeated headings to make sure they were identical. He prepared to take a screen shot to let Mel and her ISP know.

No, there was a difference between the first and second one. Oh, there were slight differences in all four. It looked like she had copied and pasted the original message to him, then added to it each time.

Without counting, Jeff knew that there were fourteen messages in total from Mel, two from the first week in September, four from the next and eight this week alone. Geez. Talk about perseveration. Did she have nothing better to do that pester him with emails? He thought she was starting a new teaching job this fall, plus taking an online class. If he knew his sister, once she got an idea in her head, she would not stop until he answered her.

Being an orderly sort, he started with the first email,

ignoring the fact that the headings on the later ones were written in all caps and ended with exclamation marks. Sometimes Mel could be melodramatic and got excited about the least little thing.

THE FIRST EMAIL'S heading was "Tip #1". It was short, thank goodness. It contained a list of things to do the day after he moved in. She used bullets and didn't bother with full sentences. Well, at least she respected his time. Her email said:

- *go get your student card (this includes getting your picture taken)*
- *go get your meal punch card*
- *go to the bookstore and buy the book we couldn't order online (your Biology lab workbook)*
- *print off a copy of your class schedule (see attachment)*
- *walk around campus to find out where all your classrooms are*
- *find quiet places on campus where you can go to be alone (try the library first)*

OKAY. Those weren't bad suggestions and Mel would likely be pleased to know that he had already done all those things. Well, except for the last one and the fourth one. Poor Mel. She had to rely on writing things down far more than he did. He didn't need to print off his schedule; he had already read it and memorizing stuff like that was easy. But, the sixth item was a good idea. Now that he read this, he remembered her talking about there being quiet spots tucked away in all sorts of places on a campus where a guy could go to find a bit of peace and quiet. She had described three such places she had found when she went to school. Yeah, he could have used some spots like that. Maybe tomorrow he'd look around. Who wouldn't appreciate a calm, quiet spot in between classes?

As if he didn't have enough on his plate right now. Jeff moved on to the second email. Its heading was Tip #2. This one's first bullet said, *"Call mom".* Whoops. He had not done that. Yeah, he remembered his mom ragging on him about remembering to call home. But he was busy. And, he had nothing he wanted to say to her or dad.

He pulled his phone out of his pocket. He carried it around with him just in case he needed to make a call. Powering it on, he saw that it was almost out of juice. He plugged it in to the charger by his keyboard and looked at the Recents in his phone log.

Mel, darn it. She was spamming his phone as well, but not nearly as many times as did his mom. He scrolled down. She had started with one call an evening, but then upped it seriously. She had even called before seven o'clock in the morning! Didn't she care that she might be waking him up? Or Phil? Geez, they were students, spending their time studying and they needed their sleep. It was a good thing that he had had his phone turned off. He was positive they didn't bug him this often when he lived at home.

~

Back to the emails. The third one's subject line read Tip #3 and it was sent during that first weekend after school started. Mel wrote:

"Now that you've gotten a taste of your classes this past week, I bet you already have some that you like and some you're not as keen on. Just wait, most of them get better. The first few lectures or so are often about giving you some of the background in that subject, teaching you some of the terminology and jargon that goes with that discipline. Still, I am sure that some classes will be more interesting than others. That happens to all of us.

But Jeff, don't go heading off in one direction, concentrating all your time and energy on just one class. Or, even two classes. Remember that you are taking five and need to devote equal time to all of them. Each one will have weekly required readings; some will have readings the prof wants done before you come to each lecture. Believe me, when they say that, they mean it. They will not just repeat what was in your text during the lecture but will assume that you've already read and understood the assigned readings and will expand on them.

Do NOT get hung up on just one class, no matter how interesting it might be. That way lies disaster and you can quickly get so far behind in your other classes that it can be tough to get caught up. You're reading this in only week two, so we know that you'll heed the warning and not get caught in that trap.

But, do write and let me know about the courses that interest you.

Love, Mel"

WELL. Wasn't that just great? *Now* she tells him after he had done just that with his Biology lab. Great.

FEELING the pressure of Mel looking over his shoulder, he pulled up the webpage for his Computer Science class. This one he was more confident about. During the first class, the prof explained that he did not take attendance; they could come or not as they choose. He hoped that they would find his lectures compelling and helpful enough that they would attend but it was not required. He would put all the slides from his lectures online where students could view them whenever they wished.

There were weekly assignments, all due on Monday mornings, and these were posted online as well. Students could read the instructions, study the examples, do the work then hand in the assignment online. All without the discomfort of leaving home. The prof even held online office hours where he would be available to answer email questions or even to have an online chat. Plus, on Friday afternoons lab assistants were present to answer any questions in the first- year computer lab.

So far, Jeff had not needed any of those methods of seeking help. The online examples were actually quite good, the text was so-so, but Google was his friend and there was lots of help to be had online for anyone with a question.

Nice that the prof made attending classes optional, because Jeff had been pretty busy in the Biology lab and in trying to find a time to eat when the cafeteria was not crowded. Good to have a considerate instructor.

Jeff checked and smiled to himself when he saw that yes, he was up to date on all the assignments for this class. All but one had been marked and you could hardly improve on the grades he had received so far. He looked closer. He wanted to know why he only received an eight out of ten on the last one. He clicked through to see the attached notes from the marker.

Darn. His code created a loop. How did he not catch that? He liked to test out each bit of code before submitting it. The marker suggested Jeff refer to the notes that he took during the September 27th lecture. Hmm. Jeff had missed that one. In fact, he had missed them all after the first one where he was given permission to not attend any more.

Was that fair? The guy says it's okay not to come, then he gives information during the lecture that is pertinent to an assignment.

Jeff scrolled over to the power point slides the prof had uploaded for that date. Oh, yeah. There. It was explained there. Jeff hadn't referred to the lecture notes because he thought he already knew enough Java Script to do the assignment. Perhaps not.

Well, everything was okay now with this class. Perhaps he might take a few moments to look at Mel's gazillion messages.

His sister's fourth email had the heading "Other Students". What? Why would she want to talk about that? Did she not have enough to do that she could muse about such extraneous things?

She wrote, "How are you finding the other students? Is this quite different than what you experienced in high school?"

And, that was it. What a strange question and what did it matter? He'd been too busy to even notice the other students in his classes or on campus. Well, other than his roommate and he was all right. And there was that guy in the Biology lab who had taken his computer place. While that was annoying, it hadn't happened again.

Come to think of it, students here *were* different from those he had known in middle school and high school. Back then, they were the reason he had dropped out of school. But here, they weren't a problem. They ignored him, which was as it should be. The odd person had asked him a question or two in the Biology lab and students worked together on problems in the Calculus seminar, but they only focused on the work. There was nothing personal about it.

Once again, Mel was right, and he did find that the students here differed from those in his high school. They must have grown up.

He read the last line of Mel's message. "Do you find that the students at college are more mature than the kids you used to go to school with? And, do you think that *you* have grown up as well?"

Mel. What a question. Of course, he had grown up. He used to be seventeen and now he was twenty. Well, duh.

THE FIFTH EMAIL was all about one thing. "Call home." Whoops. He had not done that yet even though his mom had told him to be sure and call them. When had she said? Oh, yeah, the next day after they helped him move in. Or was it when classes started? Knowing his mom, it was probably both. As if he had nothing better to do than sit on the phone making small chat. They knew that he did NOT do that. He'd been busy. He was not here to goof around but go to school. That took time.

THE NEXT EMAIL was a bit better. Mel was assuming that he wanted to know about her life because it was all about her new teaching job and the kids in her classroom. Her job was part of a special project, an experiment. She had a kindergarten class with a smaller number of students. Of the fifteen kids, seven had special needs, and four of these children had autism. There was an educational associate working with her. The progress of all fifteen kids would be tracked and their rate of learning compared to that of kids in the regular kindergarten class. In particular, the school board was interested in the academic progress of the neurotypical students.

Mel described the sensory items in the classroom, all the different seating options, the learning centers and emphasis on visuals and routines. Yeah, this would work. Jeff thought of how much better off *he* would have been in such a classroom. Mel could be annoying sometimes, but every now and then she really did know what she was talking about.

The email ended with a P.S. "Call home."

EMAIL NUMBER seven's tone changed. The heading was "Mom's bugging me". Well, welcome to the club; she often bugged him, too.

Scanning Mel's note, he saw that she had one focus in this one - call Mom. Since he had not phoned his parents, Doreen had turned her attention to Mel. Good. Share it around.

But wait. Their mother's focus was still on Jeff, but through Mel. Doreen was bugging Mel about the lack of phone calls from Jeff. Did that even make sense? While they might both be her kids, they were separate people, not even living in the same city. How was Mel supposed to *make* Jeff phone his mom?

And, if Doreen wanted to speak to him so badly, why didn't she call him herself? Oh yeah. His phone had been turned off. Now that it was powered up enough, he scrolled this his missed call log. Yep, Doreen had called him. And called and called and called. Sheesh. As if he would have wanted to talk to her that often anyway.

IN HER NEXT EMAIL, Mel again said that their mom was driving her nuts. She said that Doreen was fretting constantly because she had not heard from Jeff and worried about him.

Why would she worry? He was fine. Well, mostly fine; he thought about his focus on his Biology lab.

HE SCROLLED to the next email, but just as he feared, it was more of the same. A guy could only take so much of this stuff.

He grabbed his jacket off the back of his chair, picked up his lab notebook and headed out the door.

THE THOUGHT FLITTERED through his head that now would have been a good time to seek refuge in one of those quiet spots Mel had suggested he look for. Oh, well. Too late now.

Instead, Jeff headed for the Biology lab, the place where he had found the most success and interest in this entire campus. Funny, he had dreaded signing up for this class, certain that it would bring flooding back too many memories of high school, forced lab partners and being at the mercy of students let loose in a science lab with little to no supervision.

Just shows how a guy can change his mind. Despite that initial, awful, gasping odor the first time he'd entered the room, the work-arounds for that actually helped and he'd come to not only tolerate the smells but to look forward to the aroma of camphor and getting lost the world behind his computer monitor's portrayal of the lab material. Here he found success and peace.

Well, for a while.

CHAPTER 10

*J*eff had no idea how long he had been engrossed in his lab work. He'd listened to the lecture, watched the videos, and completed his frog dissection, and then moved on to the next lesson.

But this one gave him trouble. It wouldn't let him in. He consistently received the message that he was blocked from entering the next section of the lab course. How could that be? He had completed everything sequentially and done all of it well. His lab quiz marks were perfect or almost perfect.

Jeff logged out and looked for Agnes. He waited while she helped a couple of students locate the frog's atrium and ventricles. They needed the help of magnifying glasses. Jeff wondered at their skill level. How did they even get into this class? The parts of the heart were obvious to anyone who looked or even to anyone who had watched the videos in the lab lesson.

How could someone not transfer those images from the computer monitor into real life?

Agnes noticed Jeff. "Hi. I'll be with you in a few minutes. While I finish up here, would you mind giving them a hand?" She pointed to the counter near the window where three students were hunched over their own frog. "They are confusing the lobes of the lung with those of the liver." She smiled at Jeff's reaction to that. "This stuff doesn't come that easily to some people. Not everyone has good visual skills and that makes it tough to identify some of these organs." She returned to the students in front of her, then called over her shoulder to Jeff. "Oh, and you might want to point out the spleen and gall bladder for them as well, please."

If he wanted to? Okay, she probably didn't mean that literally. Surely she would know that that is not something he wanted to do; he had problems of his own and needed to find out how to get by the glitch in the program that was blocking his access to the next lesson. Nevertheless, he shuffled over to the counter.

The three hesitant students heard Agnes' request and waited for Jeff. He noticed that none of them had that sheen of camphor under their noses and one guy didn't even wear a mask. Well, his choice.

Jeff pulled a new pair of latex gloves from the nearby box as the students made way for him. He picked up two probes and gently moved the liver lobes to reveal the lungs hidden underneath.

"Oh, man, I don't know how you can stand to do that," said one guy.

Jeff looked at him with a question in his eyes. Really,

it didn't take any strength or skill to simply lift a couple of tiny lobes.

The guy continued. "I mean, you just dive right in there, like you're not messing around in the body of something that was once living."

What? "I *am* poking inside the body of something that was once alive. Did you think these are plastic models?"

"No, it just gives me the creeps to even think about touching this thing." He took a sniff and then coughed into his sleeve. "And, how can you stand the stink?" This was from the guy without the mask.

"First, I follow the lab rules and always wear a mask." He added, "It's required." Jeff gently lowered the liver lobes back to their natural resting place. "Then, I took Agnes' suggestion of applying a bit of camphor under my nose before putting on the mask. My roommate doesn't like the feel of the stuff right on his nose, so he rubs it on his mask, so he breathes it in that way." He looked up at the student's naked face. "You don't seem to be doing much to help yourself. No one is more sensitive to smells than me and I can stand it in here if I just follow the rules."

Next Jeff pointed out the gall bladder. One of the girls said, "I thought our gall bladders were lower down on our bodies, more toward the middle of the abdomen. My mom had to have hers removed and the incision is definitely not up there in her chest."

"You're right. We work with frogs to get an idea about organ systems. Although frogs give a good visual of the organs present in complex organisms, the organ placement is not identical in all reptiles, amphibians, and mammals. They all have their own adaptations that allow them to live successfully in their environments." Jeff continued talking about some of the adaptations that this particular species developed.

After a while he noticed Agnes standing quietly off to the side. He had no idea how long she had been listening. The students began packing up their equipment and gathering their books.

"Nicely done, Jeff. You're a good teacher. Come on over to my desk, please. I have something to ask you."

Jeff followed, saying, "I have something to ask you, too."

Agnes motioned for him to go first.

"I tried to go on to the next lesson but some glitch in the program blocked me. I can't find a way around its wall."

"I'm pretty sure I know what's happened, but let's take a look." Agnes spent a few minutes logging her credentials into the lab program, then checking the student roster. "Yes, you've completed all you can for now. The rest of the labs aren't available until after you have written and passed the midterm. That's not for another two and a half weeks."

"Is there no way around that? Could I take the midterm early so that I can get on with this work?" When Agnes shook her head no, Jeff asked, "What am I supposed to do now? Just sit here and stare at the blank monitor for the next three weeks?"

"That's what I wanted to talk to you about." She turned to face Jeff directly and pulled out a chair for him. "You were good with those students just now. I'm not sure you realize how difficult this class is for many of the people who take it. They're not really interested in going further in Biology but need this class as a science credit. Unfortunately, some of them aren't going to make it, or at least not without help. That's where you come in."

Agnes swiveled back to the computer and pulled up a notice on the student employment site. "Have you seen this?"

Jeff read the posting describing a part-time, temporary job as lab assistance for Biology 101. The job lasted from October 15th to just before final exams started in December.

"Interested?" Agnes asked.

"Not really. I have enough to do without a job. I'm here as a student, not as an employee."

"This is just a part-time job. In fact, it would require you to spend fewer hours in here than you have been for this past month or so." Jeff said nothing. "Don't you like being in this lab?"

"Yeah. But the computer program has blocked my access so I can't continue my work."

"If you *worked* here you could still spend time in the lab. You'd be helping other students just like you did today. And, you'd get paid for it."

"What about when I get access again after the midterm?"

"At the rate that you've whizzed through these lessons, you could easily keep working here and keep up with your own lab work at the same time."

"I don't know. It would mean talking to people and I do better by myself. I'm not really a people person."

"Could have fooled me," came the surprising answer. "You related very well to those students today. You gave them the knowledge they were seeking but without making them feel inadequate. It takes a sensitive person to be able to do that."

"Hah! My sister would get a laugh out of that. Me, sensitive."

Agnes spun her chair to take in the room. "Look around. There are not many students in here right now and I don't think it's very crowded when you usually come."

"I don't really notice. That's why my computer is in the corner, so I won't be bothered by other people."

"If you work here, there may be times when you are the only person in the lab. During those times you'll clean equipment, set out the apparatus needed for the next labs, or if there's nothing lab-related to do, you could sit here and do work from your other classes. But if a student asks you a question, you'd need to stop your own work and help them. And, closer to the midterm, this lab can get very crowded with students waiting in line for a turn at a computer. That's when the students who struggle with Biology or who have left the labs to the last minute all cram to get their lab assignments finished. Things get pretty hectic around here then; that's why we're advertising for a lab assistant."

Jeff's eyes flicked around the room and he shuffled from one foot to the other. "Maybe. I don't know. I don't think so. I have a lot on my mind."

"Think about it. The job's a good fit for you and would look good on your resume." Agnes attempted to be reassuring.

Jeff's movements increased. "Gotta go. There's a lot of pressure on me now."

"Well, let me know your answer. And Jeff, how are your other classes going?"

There was no answer. He was gone.

JEFF LEANED against the outside wall of the Biology building, shoulders slumped and his hands a death grip on his books. His breaths came quick and shallow. He could feel that crushing, overwhelming sensation of just too much building. First it started in his abdomen, then he could feel the pressure like a balloon growing and growing, rising and crowding out his organs until it felt like something was going to burst under the incessant, relentless, overpowering pressure.

Just then the doors burst open and the sound of thousands, no millions of voices and steps flowed by him. Some of the voices yelled, others laughed but it all reached Jeff in a garbled, cacophony of sound. Didn't they know the trauma he was going through? How could they make so much racket in the midst of his stress?

The balloon rose even higher until there was no room for his lungs to suck in air. Jeff's only thought was to flee.

At first, he ran, just ran. Somehow, the exertion of running made it easier to suck air into his squashed lungs. Gradually, the breathing part got easier and with the additional oxygen, the thinking part of his brain returned, at least long enough for him to look around. He was in a part of the campus he had never been before, the part where the veterinarian school was located.

Good thing he had spent time on Google Maps and had a fair sense of the campus. He rounded the next bend, heading back toward the main areas, his steps slowing as the sense of panic tamped down slightly. Exercise was good, even if he had taken off without that goal in mind.

Now that he was just jogging, then slowing to a quick walk, groups of students no longer parted in front of him as they heard his pounding footsteps. Now Jeff was the one to dodge and weave, all the time being careful not to brush against anyone. Wouldn't that be just what he needed at a time like this?

Up ahead was the cafeteria and those monstrous, glass windows staring down at him. He slowed his steps as he went by, eyes trailing the glass just in case anyone came toppling down from that height, causing the need to dodge the falling body.

Past it, his pace quickened as his dormitory came into sight. Taking the steps two at a time, he made it to his room, fumbled with the key, but got the door opened. His books hit the floor; his body hit the bed. He pulled the pillow from under his head and pressed it over his face, blocking out most of the light. After a few minutes, he sat up, reached for his books and placed them on his abdomen. There. The weight should help keep the size of that balloon under control. The pillow went back over his face, he turned his head to the side and slept.

THE DOOR OPENED and books hit a desk, and then Phil said, "Oh, sorry. I didn't know you were sleeping."

Jeff made no sound and no movement. He hoped Phil would just go away.

"Man, that guy never seems to go to classes," Phil muttered as he reached for the books for his next class and left, locking the door behind him.

JEFF TRIED to return to the haven of sleep, but it wouldn't work for him. He tried lying on his other side, then on his stomach, but too many images flooded his mind. And Mel's voice kept ragging on him. He might as well face the music and see what else she had written. Maybe she'd actually have something helpful to say. It had happened.

Back at his computer, Jeff hoped for some comfort. Sometimes Mel was helpful and could help ease the awful pressure inside of him.

The rest of her emails didn't look hopeful. They

started with "Call mom!" and ended with "You'll be sorry." Yeah, well there were lots of things he was sorry about.

Leaning closer, he opened the top one that had not yet been deleted. "Mom's going nuts worrying about you. Call her. You don't have to say much, just hi and that you're still alive." Did that make any sense? Of course, he was still alive if he was able to call their mother. Sheesh, Mel.

The next one tried to explain their mother's point of view. The gist of it was that Doreen was a mother - she worried. That's what mothers did. She just wanted to hear Jeff's voice say that he was okay. If Doreen didn't hear from Jeff, Mel would be unable to control the consequences. Well, that was a switch. Often Mel acted like she could organize and control everything.

She said that mom was going out of her mind with worry. Worry was a useless emotion, Jeff had learned. He'd had more than his fair share of worries and none of them did him any good. It was easy to think of all the possible things that could go wrong and all the havoc that could wreak in your life.

The possibilities were endless. But Mel had helped him to see that likely, most of these possibilities would never occur. They were dreamt up by his fertile imagination and then his mind got caught in a loop of what-ifs. The thoughts churned and churned around in his mind, providing a unique kind of torture that took hold of him and left no room for anything else. When caught in this loop, nothing productive got done. Instead, he spiraled down into a depression where he could see nothing but all the bad things that might happen.

Why didn't Mel talk about this stuff with Mom? He certainly didn't want her to feel as badly as he did when he got caught in that worry loop. Mel needed to help Mom. Next time he saw her, he'd tell her so.

IN HER NEXT MESSAGE, Mel said to call her instead of mom, then Mel could tell her she'd heard from Jeff. Or, reply to this or any of her other emails. Mel would pass on the message to mom and get her to back off. Well, at least back off somewhat. Or call dad if Jeff didn't want to talk to their mother.

That wasn't the point, Jeff thought. It wasn't that he had anything against his mother when he didn't want to talk to her. He didn't feel like talking to *anyone*. As it was, he had to speak to his roommate just to be polite. Phil wasn't bad though and he didn't ask any prying questions the way his family would.

Maybe he could reply to Mel. But, what would he say? Writing wasn't a strength for him, and it wasn't something he'd do for fun. He glanced over at the stack of books required for his English class. He'd only dropped into the class a couple times but already realized that the prof expected his students to write - every day, even. Plus, he had high expectations for the amount that a student could read. Already he was supposed to have read one novel, something by a dead guy named Hawthorne. And a bunch of poems by Emily someone. The first one was about a carriage and stopping for death - too maudlin for someone battling a depression anyway. The first year of college was stressful for students. Why would the prof want them to begin the year by reading something like that? Then, he expected them to discuss it in class. There was little point in going to a class like that.

OKAY, back to Mel's emails. The next one had a different subject line. It said, "You might not like the consequences". Well, at least it wasn't more of the same old, same old harping.

She went on to say that their mother was out of her mind with worry over Jeff. Even their dad was getting agitated about not hearing from him. Dad was usually a level type of guy and good at calming mom down. Or at ignoring her.

This time she outlined their worries specifically. Mom wondered if he was eating. Well, duh. People had to eat to live, and he was reading this, so obviously he was alive, although it had been tough those first few weeks trying to find the best times to head to the cafeteria. The problem was that it wasn't consistent. You could not guarantee that if you went every day at half past eleven, there would not be a crowd. It was the school's fault. If they would just keep regularly scheduled class hours, it would be all right but oh no, they had to change it up. On Mondays, Wednesdays and Fridays, classes began on the hour and ran for fifty minutes. But on Tuesdays and Thursdays, classes lasted for eighty minutes and began at thirty minutes past the hour. What a system. Didn't they know that life ran better when things were predictable and followed the same pattern?

Mel said that Mom also worried about Jeff's laundry. Jeff looked around at the floor. Not only was his side of the room littered with discarded clothing, but Phil's as well. Sometimes it was hard to tell the clean from the dirty stuff. Phil solved that conundrum by periodically scooping up everything he thought was his and throwing it in the washing machine. Both guys had had times when they ran out of clean underwear. Not an earth-shattering dilemma but it had caused Jeff to miss a class or two while waiting for the load to dry. Well, maybe more than two missed classes. It had been hard to develop a laundry routine. He had tried, but at the time he determined to be optimal for him, all the machines had been in use by other students. He had even taped a note to one machine that it would be in use between seven and eight that night. When he went to the laundry room at the appointed time, the machine with the note still taped to it was in use. The students in this dormitory did not seem to respect his system.

MEL WARNED Jeff that if their parents didn't hear from him soon, and *very* soon, that they might just drive down there to check up on him. Unless he wanted them camped out on his doorstep, he had better contact them or at least reply to this email.

Doorstep? He didn't even have a doorstep. He was in a dorm room. They knew that; they had been here. That didn't make sense.

His knee shook. That tic in his left eye began. Great. Mel knew just how much he hated imprecise language. As if he didn't have enough on his mind already without her adding to it.

He hit the reply button.

"Mel, what you said does not make sense. I do not live in a house and do not have a doorstep. Please edit to check for accuracy before your send emails." He hit send.

DOWN TO ONE FINAL EMAIL. It felt good to delete them as he read; now his inbox was not so cluttered.

This one started with the same yada, yada, yada, and that mom wanted reassurance that he was still in the land of the living. Yeah, well, he had replied to his sister, just a few minutes ago. She would know he was alive and could pass on that information to their parents. After all, dead men didn't send emails. So now they could all get off his back.

The rest of Mel's message talked about consequences. If he didn't contact them immediately, Mom and Dad would be driving there to check on him. And, if they didn't think he was doing well, they were prepared to drag him home. They were positive that the reason Jeff had not called home was that he was overwhelmed, in over his head and in the throes of a crippling bout of anxiety and/or depression. They were sure that this was the only reason he was not answering their calls to his cell or phoning them.

Mel thought that there might be other reasons her brother was incommunicado, but Doreen would have none of it. Yes, those other reasons had held her off the first week, less so in week two but now, there was no way Doreen would rest until she had seen for herself that her youngest child was all right.

Mel told Jeff that he needed to thank her. Mel had prevented their mother from calling the Dean and asking him to personally go check on her son. Doreen's Plan B was to call the campus security division and ask them to pay Jeff a visit. If he was not in his room when they arrived, then she would insist that a search party be organized because she imagined all manner of devious and dreadful things that could have befallen a naive young man away from home for the first time.

Naive? What was up with that?

Boy, their mother really needed to rein in her imagination. Or write a book with stories like those whirling around in her head.

When Jeff used to get caught up in all the what-ifs that could happen, Mel would tell him to get out of his own head. Go out for a walk, get some exercise, talk to people and better yet, do something for someone else.

As much as he had not felt like doing any of those things at the time, they had helped - each and every one to varying degrees for sure, but they were good suggestions. Why didn't Mel help their mother out with stuff like that?

HE REFRESHED HIS INBOX. If Mel was so anxious to hear from him, she should write him back pretty quickly. It had been many minutes since Jeff had sent her his reply. Nope, nothing yet.

He turned back to his sister's old emails. At least this was the last one, thank goodness.

Again, she told him that she can't be held responsible for the consequences. She had done her best to placate their mom and keep her calm, but since Jeff had not contacted home in all this time, their parents would likely not wait any longer. They would either call the police, which Mel had strongly urged they don't, or they would get in their car and would soon be banging on his door.

Great. As if he didn't have enough on his plate. How much worse could this day get?

CHAPTER 11

"I blame this on Mel, you know."

Hugh looked at his wife. "What does our daughter have to do with this?"

"She's been to university. She should have predicted what might happen."

"Don't I recall her warning you that Jeff might struggle while away at school?"

"That was just her getting into bossy big sister mode. You know how she gets."

Hugh knew when it was wise to say nothing. Instead, he just drove.

"THERE! You can park there, right by the door."

"The sign says, 'Emergency Vehicles Only'. This is hardly an emergency vehicle." Hugh kept going.

"If this isn't an emergency, I don't know what is,"

Doreen muttered. "You never know what shape we'll find our boy in - if we find him."

A fifty-eight-year-old man didn't roll his eyes. Or did he? Hugh was used to his wife's melodrama. It was worse when she went into mother hen mode.

"Why don't these buildings have elevators? Three floors are too many to trudge up and down all day long. No wonder Jeff is struggling."

"Doreen, first, we don't know that Jeff is struggling. Second, building codes only require elevators for structures four storeys and up. This annex of the building has only three floors. Besides, exercise is good for young people. Jeff doesn't do enough of it. Never has." He reached for his wife's hand as they rounded the landing for the second floor. She allowed his clasp for only a few steps before snatching back her hand. She was not in a mood to be comforted. She was huffing now but that would only increase after another flight. As her breathing rate rose, so did her ire.

There was a knock at the door.

Jeff was busy. After today's Calculus class and Mel's emails, he was not at his best. It penetrated just how far behind he was in these college classes. Before today he had been proud of his progress and prowess in the Biology lab, content that he really had a handle on this subject and was flying through the material. Yeah, he was doing well, but he was able to make such spectacular progress because he had ignored his other classes.

Well, not ignored, at least not consciously. He had gotten sucked into a course that he found fascinating - so much so that the others all fell away.

Why did he need to take a bunch of classes at once anyway? Why couldn't a student just concentrate on one thing at a time? Oh, yeah. That had been another suggestion of Mel's, but he had dismissed the idea. She had told him to think about going to summer school and taking just one class at a time. There would be time to get in not just one, but a second class during July and August. But who ever heard of going to school in the summer? Jeff had never done it that way in all his schooling life. School was not meant to be a July and August thing.

THE RAPPING at the door continued. Couldn't whoever was there figure out that he was busy? It was rude to keep interrupting a guy who was trying to get a handle on his classes.

Jeff donned his noise-cancelling headphones, put on some Lindsay Stirling music, and pulled up the Computer Science class website.

Mel slumped at her desk. It was the end of the school day and all the little ones had vacated the premises. How could she feel exhilarated and exhausted at the same time?

Mustering her energy reserves, she stood to straighten the room before the janitor came in to do his thing. All the little chairs were already upside down on the tables, hanging by their seats. Mel thought that this was one of the routines her students enjoyed the most.

Although the children took care of the regular chairs, there were many seating options in the room that were not amenable to being hoisted by small hands. The therapy balls were too prone to running away, being kicked or tossed. Mel moved these balls to the center of the tables, along with the inflatable peanut chairs and some of the rings that held the therapy balls in place.

Back in university, she remembered one instructor saying that kindergarten was the most difficult class to teach. Today, Mel agreed with her. This was not her first experience with kindergarten, but this class was different. So much was riding on how this year went - well, mainly how Mel performed. Yes, that was the right word because she did feel like a performer. Part of the agreement for this experimental classroom was that there would be an open-door policy. Any parent, teacher, board member or, it felt like almost anyone in the world, could drop in at any time to observe Mel and her kids.

They wanted proof that it was money well spent to give her only fifteen instead of the half dozen more students usually placed in kindergarten rooms. They wanted proof that having almost as many special needs students as typical kids in the room was a good idea. Would *those* kids take up so much of the adult attention that the typical kids would be neglected? In these days of standards and data collection would it be possible to show the progress of each and every member of the class?

To make this trickier, Mel had refused to hand-pick her special needs students. She took the first seven whose parents applied. Cherry-picking her collection of students would surely have given her the results the school board hoped for, but that wouldn't be realistic nor representative of what might happen in future years. Mel preferred that this study be based on a random selection. The only criteria she had set was that at least four of the students have a diagnosis of an autism spectrum disorder.

Kids with autism seemed to be garnering the most attention in their school district. Teachers were saying they didn't know how to teach kids with these types of needs nor how to include them in their regular classrooms. Mel was not a fan of strictly segregated classrooms that lumped all the kids with autism together in one room all day.

Like any kindergarten teacher, Mel's initial goal was to teach the kids routines. When some of the students are autistic, establishing these routines was even more critical.

Thank goodness for Laurie, the educational associate assigned to Mel's classroom. Just as she had wanted the students in the room to be as randomly chosen as possible, she had made the same request about the EA. Teachers did not get to choose the EA who would work with them; Mel wanted that same policy to apply to her classroom. No one would be able to say that this experiment had worked because Mel was able to pick and choose either the staff or the students.

Luckily, the two of them clicked and got onto each other's wavelengths within the first couple weeks. They had similar ideas on the need for developing consistent routines. Even though Mel had set up her classroom over the summer and thought she had all her routines firmly in place, Laurie suggested a few tweaks that actually worked better. Sometimes two brains can come up with more strategies than any one person could have imagined.

They also approached the kids in a similar fashion - quiet, relaxed, open but firm. They spent hours those first couple of weeks getting to know their students, then setting up tentative learning plans for each child, knowing full well that these plans were works in progress that would be tweaked and re-written many times during the year. These initial plans gave them a blueprint to use when talking to the parents and a baseline of skills the kids demonstrated coming into the classroom.

Yes, it had been a lot of work so far, but that's always how it was at the start of the school year. Getting to know the kids, establishing routines and expectations, turning a bevy of highly individual personalities into a working group, ready to play and learn together.

While Mel loved her students and enjoyed Laurie's company, right now she was relishing the quiet of having the classroom all to herself. Having stayed late so many days already, Laurie was due some time off and had left with the children after the last bell.

Mel kicked off her shoes, wiggled her toes, clasped her arms and stretched them high above her head. The energy of five-year-olds was infectious but right now she was glad that class was over for the day.

She booted up her computer; time to catch up on some emails.

First, she checked for any messages from the parents of her students. It was key to keep in close touch at the beginning of the year as they were getting to know one another and building trust. Only one today - Jenny had a dental appointment tomorrow and wouldn't be at school until the latter part of the morning. Mel made a note of this, checked her day planner to see what they would be doing around that time and quickly made up a visual to show Jenny where she should be and what her task was. Task was really a misnomer. Mel's classroom learnings were heavily play-based. The kids thought they were having fun, and they were. But each play center was carefully designed to introduce a concept or reinforce a new learning, all the while building social and language skills.

There was one email from her principal, Dr. Hitkins. Mel appreciated the fact that Dr. Hitkins never wasted staff meeting time with straight forward information that could be shared in an email.

She had received a few emails from supply companies, hoping to interest her in classroom materials. That would be nice, but with budget constraints, she had spent pretty much her whole allotment just getting the room set up. Still, it was helpful to look through these catalogs for ideas. Plus, she could dream, couldn't she?

Oh! Well, looky, looky. There was an email from Jeff. She looked closer. Perhaps not the type of email she had been hoping for, but at least it was a reply. Her brow furrowed as she scrolled through her Sent folder, looking at all the messages she had sent to Jeff these past few weeks. Well, one reply was better than no reply. She returned to the reading pane. She was able to read Jeff's entire message without the need to even open the email. The brief reply said, "Mel, what you said does not make sense. I do not live in a house and do not have a doorstep and am not camping. You know that I don't like camping and neither does mom. You need to edit for accuracy before you send emails."

She had to scroll back to see what he was talking about. She had written to him so many times that she had forgotten the content of that particular message. Oh, yeah. She smiled to herself. That's the one where she had threatened that their parents were about to camp on Jeff's doorstep if they didn't hear from him.

If he were here, she knew that Jeff would complain to her about her imprecise language or over reliance on idioms. He had a broad category of expressions that he classed as idioms.

But at least he had replied. This was proof that he had read at least some of her messages and that he was alive.

She rummaged in her purse for her cell to let their mother know that finally she had heard from Jeff. The house phone rang and rang; she tried the cell. A mechanical voice told her that the cell number she tried to reach was not available.

JEFF GOT QUITE A BIT DONE. This Computer Science stuff really wasn't that bad once you got into it. Although he had not attended any lecture or lab past the first class, the online lectures were helpful. Some of the assignments were useless, in Jeff's opinion, so he left those until last. But some were a challenge and he even learned some stuff. It took all the rest of the afternoon, but he got caught up with this class - well, as caught up as he wanted to be, leaving out the more pointless assignments. Good. Now they were done and stored on his computer.

A warning from Mel rang in his ear. She had lectured him about learning the peculiarities of each prof, because they might want assignments handed in in different ways and to pay attention to each assignment's due date.

Well, he would worry about that later.

CHAPTER 12

"You must!"

The fellow in the uniform regarded Doreen. "There is nothing I *must* do except follow the rules of my job, lady." He looked at Hugh. "Or what my wife tells me to do."

"Our son could be dead in there and no one would know. He could be hurt and needing us."

"How old is your kid?"

"Almost twenty."

"Then he's an adult and gets to do what he wants. Some of the tales I could tell you about what these kids get up to here…."

"I don't care about those other kids and besides, our son's not like that. He's a good boy, quiet and responsible."

Hugh regarded his wife. Calmly, he said, "I think you might be shooting yourself in the foot with that one."

The security guard picked up on it. "If he's so responsible, why are you trying to check up on him?"

"Look, our son's disabled. He's not like other young men."

"What's he doing here, then?"

"He has the right to attend college just like anyone else."

"Lady, I'm confused. Look, I can't open anyone's dorm door without a good reason. Those reasons include the possibility of harm to a person or property. Or overdue fees. Neither of the guys in that room are behind in their payments. You're going to need to bring me something else before I can open their door for you.

"Have you tried calling him?"

That set Doreen off on all that they'd tried over the last month and a half.

Hugh tugged on her arm. "Come on. This is getting us nowhere. Let's thank the good gentleman for his time then go find someone who can help us."

"You might try counselling services," the guard yelled as they walked away.

HE WAS RIGHT. Sort of. It would have been easier if Jeff had registered with Disability Services. As it was, he was unknown to them. The Disability office explained the types of assistance they could provide if a student chose to self-declare as a person with a disability. He could receive extra time for assignments and exams, have his tests spaced out, receive tutoring assistance, help with note taking, regular study groups and social gatherings as well as mentors who would help him keep on track with his course work. All of those sounded like things that might help Jeff.

"Well, sign him up then. This is exactly what he needs," directed Doreen.

No, they wouldn't. Or, couldn't. The catch was that since Jeff was an adult, he got to decide what he needed, and *he* had to have come to Disability Services requesting help; his parents could not do it for him.

Frustrated, they left in search of the counselling offices. Maybe Jeff had talked to someone there, someone who knew him and understood that he might be in trouble.

That office was also of little help. They refused to confirm or deny any knowledge of Jeff due to confidentiality issues. They would only be able to discuss his status with his parents if Jeff had given his written consent for them to do so.

They could help with security and getting into Jeff's room if there was concrete evidence that their son might be at risk. Had there been a suicide note? Had he spoken to them or written to them about the possibility of harming himself? Had he told them that he felt threatened by anyone?

Again, Doreen started in on the inability to contact Jeff all these weeks. Unfortunately, it didn't appear that he was the only student on campus who chose to be autonomous and wasn't speaking to his or her parents as often as the older generation would prefer.

They left. "Our next stop is the police," Doreen informed her husband.

He sighed. "Don't you think that's a little drastic? Do you want him to have a record?"

"How could he have a record? He's never done anything wrong. We need help and there's no place left to turn."

"Let's head back to his room. Maybe we'll catch him coming or going from class. He can't stay in his room forever. Or maybe we'll run into Phil." He checked his watch. "It's almost noon. Maybe one of the boys will be stopping by for lunch. Jeff likes to eat; let's go to the cafeteria and see if we catch him there."

Doreen wrinkled her nose at the offerings at the hot food section of the cafeteria line. "Not as good as my cooking," she said. "This stuff will make Jeff put on weight. Look at that grease. Oh, this is not the kind of food that our boy is used to."

"Keep it quiet, please, Doreen. Just nod and take it and pretend that you like it. You don't see the kids here complaining, do you?" They were part of a long line making its way through the serving area. Although there were other options, fries seemed to make their way onto most plates.

They took their trays to seats near the wall-to-ceiling windows. The view was magnificent, and from there they could see the walkways that converged on the cafeteria building. "Jeff must love this view."

Hugh looked at her. "How could you say that? You know that Jeff is leery of heights, always has been. Even going up the stairs, he stays near the wall rather than the open railing side."

"Oh, well that was when he was younger. He grew out of all that."

Hugh had learned years ago that there was no point in arguing some things. His wife's view of reality was fixed. Instead, he kept his eyes on the entrance to the cafeteria.

The food wasn't all that bad, he thought. If Doreen gave it a chance, she might see that it was nice to have a break from cooking occasionally. As it was, he had to drag her out the few times they went to a restaurant. There was always something wrong with the food or the service.

There. Hugh half stood. Wasn't that Phil, his son's roommate coming in? They'd only met once, on that first day, but it looked like him. He went after him mumbling, "Be right back," to his wife.

"Phil?" What was the kid's last name? He called again and the boy turned to look over his shoulder.

After a moment of confusion, Phil's face cleared. "Mr. Nicols? Hi, how are you?" They shook hands.

"We're fine, fine, thanks. Just here to pay a visit to our son. Have you seen him?"

"Not since this morning when I left for class. Jeff was still sleeping." His face colored; he did not want to get his roommate in trouble. "We have different schedules so don't always leave at the same time." Like hardly ever.

"I remember what that's like." There was an awkward pause. "So how is Jeff?" There was no easy way to ease into this.

"Fine, I guess. I don't know, we don't talk about stuff like that, just about classes and such." Phil's puzzled look was back. "Why is there a problem?" He did not want to get into something between Jeff and his parents. He had enough dealing with his own family, even though they were mostly okay.

"No, no problem. It's just that we hadn't heard from him in a while and we had some free time, so we thought we'd drive down to see how things are going. Maybe take him out for lunch, you know." Then he added, "You're welcome to join us, of course."

"Thanks, but I'm eating here and have a class right after."

"Well, come and join us. Jeff's mother will be glad to see you." Will she ever. Hugh almost felt sorry for Phil.

TRYING TO HIDE HIS RELUCTANCE, Phil carried his tray to the window.

"Phil! How lovely to see you." Doreen could turn on the charm. She chit chatted away, learning more about the young man who shared a room with her boy. You'd think that she was simply genuinely interested in Phil, rather than trying to glean information about Jeff.

Phil was equally as cagey, trying to remain polite yet spill none of what might be Jeff's secrets. How he wished that Jeff would suddenly appear, letting Phil make his excuses to leave.

A glance at his watch gave him relief. "I really have to go now. I have to get my books before this next class. It was nice seeing you again." He stood and tried to get away.

Doreen was quick. She had their trays in hand, ready to follow Phil to the conveyor belt, then out the door. With a friendly smile, she said, "We'll come with you. We're about to go meet Jeff anyway." Behind Phil's back, she signaled to Hugh to hurry and keep up.

Before inserting his key in the door, Phil turned back to his roommate's parents. "Ah, I should warn you. We weren't expecting company, so neither of us has cleaned up. There's well, stuff all over." He hastened to add, "It's not as bad as it looks. We know where everything is, and we don't get it mixed up. It just looks messy. Unorganized." Dirty, he was thinking. And it might stink a little. He tried to remember when either of them had last done laundry or if the clothes on the floor were dirty or clean. Oh well, not his parents.

It was dark in the room with the drapes still shut. The light from the hallway illuminated only part of one bed, Phil's. It was unmade but at least it wasn't strewn with underwear or anything embarrassing.

There was a lump under the covers on the other bed. Jeff, with a pillow over his head. The guy didn't go to many classes and certainly not morning ones. Phil rustled through the lopsided stack of books and papers on his desk, hastily grabbed what he hoped was the right textbook. He'd better get out of here before whatever went down between Jeff and his parents. With a quick, "See ya," he left, shutting the door behind him.

SILENCE. Hugh's and Doreen's eyes went from each other to the form on the bed and back again. "Should we just go?" whispered Hugh.

"No way. I didn't come all this way without talking to our boy, seeing if he's all right. I've woken him up before and I'll do it again." She grabbed Jeff's blanket-clad foot and shoved it. No response. She wiggled it back and forth.

"Phil, what's wrong with you?" A muffled voice came from under the pillow.

"It's not Phil. This is your mother."

Not in his dreams. His mother's voice was never in his dreams. Jeff pulled the pillow down and blinked. Doreen marched over and pulled back the curtain, letting in the mid-day sun. How many times had this happened in his life?

"What are you doing in bed, young man?"

"Mom give me a break. I'm tired."

"Doreen," began Hugh.

"No, don't Doreen me. I want to know why our son is still in bed at one o'clock in the afternoon. Jeff?"

"I was up late. I'm tired."

"Maybe we should go Doreen and come back in a

while. Give Jeff time to wake up and make himself presentable."

"After all it took to get us in here? I am *not* leaving until I get some answers."

Hugh turned his back on them, picked up a biology textbook and rifled through it.

Doreen started in on their son, demanding to know why he had not phoned them or responded to their messages.

As he put the book down to look at another, Hugh spotted a set of keys beside Jeff's computer. An idea took hold. He held them up. "Jeff, are these the keys to your room?"

Jeff squinted in in his direction. "Yeah."

"How about your mom and I leave to give you a chance to get dressed. We'll be back in half an hour." Both Jeff and Doreen needed time to get themselves together. He pocketed the keys.

Dressed, but looking worse for wear, Jeff glanced at his parents as keys rattled in the lock, and then the door opened.

"How'd you get in?" he asked. He glanced at the corner of his desk. "Oh, yeah."

Doreen towered over her son. "Why didn't you answer our calls? Why didn't you let us know how you were?"

"Geez, mom. Leave me alone. It's early."

Hugh could see his wife's blood pressure rising.

Really. It was a thing with her, starting with the flush to her cheeks.

Doreen began gathering up clothes. "Pack your things. You're coming home with us."

"What? Mom, I've got classes." He noticed what she was doing. "Hey, leave my stuff. What are you doing?"

"You're obviously not doing well. You need to be home where we can look after you. I worried that this might happen, but oh no, your sister said it would be fine."

That's not how Hugh recalled the conversations, but now might not be the right time to correct her.

"Where's your suitcase? Let's get these things gathered up."

"I'm not going anywhere. Can't you see I'm working?"

It went on, each getting louder. Hugh did what he had often done - intervene without either party thinking he was taking sides or butting in. "Jeff, let's go get something to eat."

"But you just…." began his wife.

"We passed a pancake place not far from here. Come on, son."

Pancakes were Jeff's weak spot. All his life he'd been a sucker for them, and Hugh had used that when he needed to separate his wife from his son. It worked every time. Both were more reasonable after a cooling off period. Well, a little more reasonable anyway.

The coffee gave Jeff the jolt he needed to wake up.

"Want to tell me about it, son?"

"What's to tell?"

"Your mom and I were worried, not hearing from you in so long."

"It didn't feel like long to me. You were just here."

"Yes, we were. Six weeks ago. We have not heard from you since then. That's a long time for a worried mom when her youngest leaves home for the first time."

"I was fine. I *am* fine."

That was debatable but again, now was not the time. "If you say so, but *we* didn't know that. How could we?"

"You could have assumed. I'd have let you or Mel know if I needed something."

"Jeff, I'm not trying to interfere in your life…"

Jeff looked at him.

"Well, maybe a little. But I wouldn't have if you had just dropped us a line."

"What? Dad, it's a little early in the morning to be talking in riddles. Say what you mean."

"You're right. We needed to hear from you - to hear that you're all right, to hear what you thought of college and how it was going. We worry."

"I'm fine, I told you."

"We're parents. Parents worry; it's our job. We're used to seeing you every day. We miss you and are interested in your life, so we want to know how things are and what you're up to."

"Sounds kind of nosy."

"Maybe, but that's what families do. They're interested in each other's lives and keep in touch with each other." He paused a moment. "That 'drop a line' thing. I meant we need you to send us a text, an email or phone us. It doesn't have to be long, just a sentence or two so that we hear from you and know that you're all right. This moving out is a big deal for you, let alone having a new roommate and being a student again.

"I know that your last student experiences in high school did not go so well for you. I wanted to know how it was this time."

Jeff's shoulders lowered. It seemed that the attack mode was over, or at least that's how it felt to him.

"It's okay. It's not like high school. Everyone leaves me alone here, no more of that bullying stuff. I'm careful and I watch but it's not the same. Maybe everyone's grown up and doesn't do that shit anymore."

"I'd like to think that this is true but I'm not sure. Still, I'm glad that you've not run into any trouble here."

"Not *that* kind of trouble, anyway."

That got Hugh's attention.

"What kind of trouble? Do you have enough money?"

"Yeah, money's fine. I made lots from those coding gigs and saved most of it, so I'm okay. My fees are all paid for the semester so there's not much to pay for."

"And?"

"Nothing."

Hugh regarded his youngest child. Jeff knew that look.

"It's the classes."

Hugh waited. Jeff was not going to wiggle out of this.

"Some are okay." He warmed to the topic. "Biology is going great! I'm way ahead in my work. I did so well in the labs that they offered me a job - I'm helping other students. Some of them just don't get it, even the simplest things, and I need to show them over and over. The labs are all independent work and I guess some people aren't good at being self-motivated."

Hugh raised an eyebrow. "And?"

"I didn't think I'd like Biology; it sounded too much like what I went through in high school. Mel made me sign up for it, saying that I had to have a science and to keep an open mind. I didn't, but I got hooked on it anyway. The labs are really cool; it's way more interesting than I thought it could be, nothing like we took in high school."

"Another thing not like high school is how classes are. It might be easier if you just started at nine o'clock and went all day but it's not like that here. Classes are spread out, all at different hours and scattered all over the campus. Ya gotta move from building to building. There are no bells or buzzers to tell you when it's ten minutes before class starts so you know you need to get to the next room. They expect you to do stuff like that on your own. I'm not that good at paying attention to time.

"Then there's the work."

"Is it hard for you?"

"Nah. Or most of it isn't anyway. It's just that they keep throwing stuff at you. You think that you got caught up in one subject, then you're way behind in another. It's like they think that you have nothing to do but work on their stuff."

His dad's other eyebrow went up.

"Yeah, I know. That's what I'm here for. But I'm used to doing my own things as well. I've got things to do and it's hard to get it all done."

"That's what your mother and I worried about. You've got the brains, son, we know that. But the organization part, the keeping track of time and what needs to be done in the various classes can be hard. That's what Mel was trying to tell you about.

"If you'd contacted us, we maybe could have helped you through some of this. You know, like ways to organize things and keep on top of your workload."

Jeff put down his fork. "I get it, Dad. I was just so busy and then I got behind even when I thought I was doing well, then there was all this pressure, then I saw all the messages from you and mom and Mel and how was I ever going to answer each one when I had all this other work to do?"

Hugh laughed. "We didn't expect you to respond to every single message. Just one or two would have been fine."

He thought a moment. "Look, why don't we have a system. Put a reminder on your phone or computer that says once a week you'll contact us. A phone call, a text, or an email; any one is fine. You pick the time and when the reminder comes up, you contact us. We'll expect that once a week and won't bug you as long as we hear from you weekly. Deal?"

"Yeah, I guess that would work."

"Good. Now there's something else I wanted to talk to you about. Next week is Reading Week."

"What's that? Some national holiday where we're all supposed to read? I read enough as it is. These textbooks are huge and I'm reading all the time."

"Reading Week is a break the college gives. You're not the only student here who finds the workload overwhelming. They give you a week off from classes during Reading Week and students use that week to get caught up. Midterm exams are coming up and it's a chance to get prepared for them."

"A week off from classes is okay. I wonder about the bio lab though and how much work I need to do there."

"Here's what I propose, son. Come home with us now. It's Thursday and you'll only miss one day of classes. Let your mother fuss over you for a while. It will keep her happy."

"You always say, 'a happy wife is a happy life;'."

"You got that right and these last few weeks have been tough with her worrying about you."

"Sorry. I didn't think."

"Bring all your work with you and spend this next week relaxing at home and getting caught up. I'm sure that Mel would be willing to help you get sorted out and to give you some tips on staying on top of things."

"I'll bet." A blessing and a curse.

Hugh grinned. "Let's go collect your mother and your stuff, and then be on the road."

IT AFFRONTED HER. Everything, absolutely every little thing about this room offended Doreen's sense of right and order. From the smell, to the partially opened drapes to the total disarray, it was all wrong, so wrong.

How could anyone live this way? How could the boys work amid such mass confusion?

Well, she was here now and could do something about it. The poor lads were so busy with their schoolwork that they didn't have time to pick up after themselves. Some things a mother did better. She could make order out of this chaos.

IT WASN'T AS easy as she anticipated. For one thing, at home she was used to moving about the basement, gathering Jeff's dirty clothes from the floor. But here, two boys resided, seemingly equally poor at using either dresser drawers or hangers.

She began with the assumption that the mess on the right side of the room belonged to her son and on the left would be Phil's things. She went in search of laundry facilities and found the machines at the other end of the hallway. Poor boys. If only the washers and dryers were closer to their room, they might have a better chance of keeping tidy. At least there were machines open. Now, where was that nice laundry hamper she bought for Jeff?

Not until she'd used his pillowcase as a collector of dirty clothes did she find the hamper in the corner under his bed. Perhaps getting him a collapsible one was not the best choice. She loaded two washers with Jeff's clothes and bedding then returned to the room to straighten up. Again, it was a hard call because there seemed to be some overlap, but she assumed that everything on or near Jeff's desk belonged to him. How could the dear boy concentrate with papers and books strewn all over? At least if she tidied things into piles it would give him more desk room to work on. So many loose pieces of paper. If she could put some organization into this, it would help him a lot.

As she worked on Jeff's desk and bedside table, her eyes strayed often to Phil's side of the room. Obviously, his mother had not been here, or his things would not be in such disarray. College was hard on young people; there was so much to do and so little time.

Since she was here anyway and had to wait for Jeff and Hugh's return, she might as well give her son's friend a hand. Again, using a pillowcase as a carrier, she gathered up the clothes from Phil's half of the room, stripped the bed and started two more washing machines. It was hard to tell dirty clothes from clean ones that may have found their way to the floor, but when she was finished with them, they'd all be presentable and neatly put away.

Wouldn't the boys be pleased?

CHAPTER 13

They took their sweet time over coffee, Doreen thought, but while they were gone she had plenty of time to make improvements in the boys' dorm room. They would not recognize it when they got back. She could imagine how grateful they'd be.

THE DOOR WAS PROPPED open with a pail and attached wringer. The slosh of water sounded as they approached his room, then the pail received a shove into the hallway.

Hugh peered in the doorway. "Doreen! For the love of…".

"What? What's she doing, dad?" Jeff pushed by and froze. This wasn't his room. What was his mother doing in someone else's room? He backed out and looked at the number beside the door frame.

Hugh's hand tightened on his arm. "Take it easy, Jeff. You know she was just trying to help." But this time she'd gone too far.

"What the hell are you doing? Where's my stuff? My clothes?" Then he spied his desk, or what used to look like his desk. "My stuff! All my notes! They're gone. How am I going to find anything now?"

"It's all here, Jeff. Look, I organized it. It's all in piles now, sorted according to size when I couldn't figure out which subject each one went with. Isn't it so much better?" She beamed.

Sensing impending disaster, Hugh slipped his arm over his wife's shoulders, steering her toward the door. "Let's let Jeff get his things together. He's coming home with us for the week."

"You're leaving?" Phil's shoulders filled the doorway. "Sorry," he apologized to Hugh and Doreen. "I didn't mean to eavesdrop. I was coming to get my books for my last class." Then, to Jeff, "You heading out? You're coming back, aren't you?" Then he looked past the parents toward Jeff's desk. "Whoa. I can see your desktop. You really are packing things up."

"No, that was me." Doreen took the credit.

Phil looked between Mrs. Nicols and Jeff. He knew how *he'd* feel is anyone messed with his desk. His piles had meaning, and he knew how to put his hands on anything he needed.

Jeff stood staring at his tidy desk. No words came.

Phil glanced at the rest of the room. It was not recognizable as theirs. "You must have packed up everything you own," he told Jeff. Then he noticed the lack of clothes on the floor. "Hey, did you take some of my stuff, too?"

"Oh, no, silly, he wouldn't do that." Doreen smiled broadly. "I cleaned for him, did the laundry and put everything away in its place.

"When I'd finished, I realized how messy your side of the room looked. You've been so busy with studying that you have had no time to look after your things and your mother isn't here, so I did it for you."

Hugh slapped a palm to his forehead. "Doreen! You didn't!"

Phil gawked. And gawked. "You touched my stuff?"

Doreen nodded, pleased with herself.

"I had dirty things on the floor. Even my underwear!"

"Oh, I know, dear. I've lived with men for thirty years and I know how you can be about leaving your clothing on the floor. I've picked up after Jeff and his father for years.

"You'll find all your clothes cleaned and folded and in your drawers or hanging in the closet. Some of your drawers were empty, so it was hard to tell where you put stuff. So, I stored everything in the most logical places. They'll be easy for you to find." She spread her arms. "There. Doesn't this place look so much better now? The room even looks bigger with everything in its place."

Taking his wife by the arm, he propelled her out the

door. Over his shoulder he sent a silent apology to Phil, adding, "She means well." He knew that counted little after this invasion of privacy. "It won't happen again."

Silence filled the room. Jeff, lost in his own head after seeing the destruction his mother caused.

Phil came in, inspected the floor between their beds that was devoid of, well, anything. He stood over his desk with is books now in a neat pile, arranged with the largest text on the bottom. His headphones, with the cord neatly wrapped around the head band sat atop the top edge of his monitor. The note papers he had scattered across the desktop were now stacked together There weren't so many of them that he couldn't sort through to find what he wanted, but still. How dare she? Jeff wouldn't touch his stuff; they never interfered with each other, respecting each other's privacy and space. Wasn't that what adults did?

His blood boiled. But the cause of his angst was no longer present, and he could hardly take it out on Jeff. Apparently, they'd left Doreen alone here while Jeff and his dad were out. That was enough time for her to do her worst.

Worst. His dirty underwear. His briefs. Even *he* didn't want to touch them. What was *wrong* with this woman?

He wracked his mind over what else he might have had laying around. It was one thing to have a guy roommate, one who wasn't too picky, but to have that guy's *mother* privy to all his secrets? Not that he had anything too nasty lurking, but he could have. Would have served her right if she'd gotten an eyeful of something she wouldn't have wanted to see.

Still, his ire needed a place to vent. Looking at Jeff, he reined it in. This wasn't Jeff's fault; he couldn't help being born to that woman and he obviously had not told her to clean up. Clean. Yeah, the place did look better, but they would have gotten around to it some time. It didn't really bother either of them the way it was.

A run. He needed a run. Screw class. He needed to get out of here. But where were his running shorts? Where would that woman have put his stuff? Rummaging produced the clothes he wanted and, ripping off his jeans, he got ready. It was kind of nice not to have to give things the sniff test before deciding if he could wear them, but still.

He grabbed his keys. Oh yeah, Jeff was leaving. The guy still looked like he was in a trance. "Hey," Phil called.

No response.

"Hey, Jeff, are you all right?" The guy really looked traumatized by what his mother had done to him. To them both.

Jeff's head shook slightly and then he turned. "Yeah. Sorry, man. I'm sorry for what my mom did to you. I didn't see that one coming. I had no idea when I left to get lunch with my dad that she would destroy our room. I'm really sorry that she did this to you, too." He looked around the place. "It won't happen again. I won't let her and neither will dad."

Phil sighed. "It's all right, man. It was a shock, seeing the place like this and knowing that she'd pawed through my things." He pulled back from going there. Jeff looked tormented enough. "You're leaving?"

"Since my folks came all the way down there, I guess I'll go back with them now and stay home for Reading Week."

"But you're coming back?"

CHAPTER 14

*A*h, home.

It didn't take Jeff long to settle in. It was almost like he'd never left, and the last six weeks at college had never happened. In many ways it was a relief. Home was familiar. Home was safe. Home was predictable.

Back in the basement, he could do what he'd done for the last few years. Getting lost in the world of his computer felt comfortable.

DOREEN HUMMED as she worked in the kitchen. With Jeff home, she was busy, busier than she had been in almost two months. Making her son's favorite foods filled a need in her, a need to care for her family.

"Hugh," she called. "Why don't we buy Jeff a small freezer. That way I can make extra food to send back with him. Then he can just heat up a portion rather than having to go eat those nasty cafeteria meals."

Hugh leaned against the doorway to the kitchen. "Really? You think that might work?"

"Jeff's not much for cooking but he can surely put something in the oven or use a microwave. I'll pack things up in single serving meals. He can store them in his freezer then, next time he's home, I'll have another load ready for him to take back."

"A freezer. Where do you think he'd put it? You've been in his room; you're probably more familiar with it now than either of the boys are. You could not fit one more thing in their dormitory." He shook his head. "No, we're not trying to shove a freezer in there. Nor a microwave."

Yeah, that was right. Well, it was a good idea and would have been so nice for her boy. She could even have prepared enough that he could share with Phil. Such a nice boy.

OBLIVIOUS TO HIS mother's attempts at further planning his life, Jeff's headphones blocked out all noise. Even though this was the same computer he used while away at school, somehow it felt different here in his basement. More like it was supposed to. He played the same game that he'd spent hours on in his dorm, but it was better here. Jeff liked things he was used to.

The computer pinged. The timer on the corner of his monitor screen flashed its zeros. How irritating. Mel had insisted he install this productivity app on his machine. It was supposed to let him work unhindered for twenty minutes straight, then it would reset for a five-minute break, then back to another twenty-minute work stint. After two cycles of this, he'd get a ten-minute break.

As irritating as that ping was, when he worked on coding contracts, it had actually helped. Mostly. Knowing he had just that brief twenty minutes made his brain work harder. But sometimes, when he was really into things, he hated the interruption. He'd set it to on mode now while he played games because he thought he might take a look at some of his school stuff. He knew that he could get lost in games for hours and hours. But this was fun. He shut off the timer.

JEFF RELAXED AT HOME. It was good to regroup and rest up. Not that he slept all that much. It was easy to slip back into his old routine of staying up most of the night on his computer and sleeping in until mid-afternoon. There was no worry about needing to hit the cafeteria before lunch service was over as Mom gladly prepared food whenever he ventured upstairs. Here he didn't even have to load his dirty dishes onto a tray and take them to the conveyor belt.

The only annoying thing was Mel. He guessed that siblings were always like that, getting on each other's nerves. She'd left messages for him, texted and emailed. She was at it again. When did she think he had the time to respond to all of them?

But she was coming over tonight, or at least that's what their mom said. Probably wanting to rag on Jeff about something or other.

Another message flashed on his screen. It only showed him the first couple lines, but it was Mel. Again. He peered closer. It was something about organizing and college classes. Yeah, she'd probably ask him about that tonight.

Maybe he'd take a look and impress her with what he knew.

It was time. The break had been good, but he had stuff to do. Nice that they gave students a week off to get caught up. He looked at what was needed for his comp sci class. Quite a bit, actually. Well, he had time to get those assignments knocked off. He had all week.

He glanced at the date and time in the corner of his computer screen. Thursday, October 29th. Thursday! Classes began again on Monday. That was just three days away! How had that happened?

He'd messed it up. Badly. He was so behind in some

classes. That's what this week off was for, Mel said - to get caught up. He looked at his computer's clock. Crap! He'd already been home for seven days and had not looked at any of his schoolwork. Once back in the basement, he did what he'd always done there. It was all good and productive, or fun stuff, but none of it had anything to do with his courses. Two days left, then one day of driving. That was it, then he needed to be back in his dorm. If he returned.

He could feel the signs that all was not well. His shoulders rose closer to his ears. His jaw clenched and his fists tightened. He knew that when those things happened, his heart rate sped up and his breathing changed. Breaths were not something he gave any thought to most of the time, but training with Mel had taught him that these were signs of tension and when his body responded like this, his breathing changed from a regular rhythm that required no thought, to shallow, rapid intakes of air. Everything compounded each other. The faster his breathing, the more rapid his heartbeat, not allowing his body to relax. The more tense his muscles, the shorter his breaths and the faster his heart worked. No good. From there it was only a short stroll to anxiety, the kind that could leave him paralyzed.

He hated feeling that way. When he practiced with Mel, he could lower his heart rate and breathe more deeply and slowly, helping his body to relax. But that was during practice sessions. It was much harder to employ the techniques when he was stressed.

Now, he had good reason to be stressed. All this

work to do and just two more days to get it all done. He had the nights as well, of course, but he should sleep sometime.

His knee bounced up and down. His fingernails cut into his palms leaving marks that he didn't even notice. He didn't have time to work on relaxation exercises. He had too much to do. But the more he thought about his assignments, the more his tension rose until it began to drive out rational thought. He couldn't think when he felt like this, couldn't make plans. He needed to find a way to get calmer.

He closed his Computer Science class site; he'd have to worry about this when he was feeling better, more in control. Instead, he pulled up a game - not the one he'd been playing but an older one, one in which he used to escape when the pressures around him seemed too great.

Soon he was mesmerized by the flashing images on his screen. His fingers unclenched, then faster and faster they pounded the keys while his right hand clutched the mouse, moving it with unerring accuracy and speed.

SHE GAVE HIM A HUG. Jeff didn't really mind Mel's hugs. His sister understood. Her hugs were brief and firm - none of that awkward lingering or gentle caressing that rubbed his skin the wrong way.

She seemed genuinely pleased to see him. Jeff didn't mind her coming over, although she could have picked a better time. How could she forget that he had all kinds of work to do and precious little time in which to complete it?

Supper consisted of far too much food than any four people could be expected to consume. For each bowl that she placed on the table, Doreen said, "It's your favorite, Jeff." Yeah, he liked these foods, but how could each one be his favorite? The word 'favorite' implied one, or maybe a couple of things, but how could anyone call these many things one person's favorite? He opened his mouth to clarify the point.

His shin took a jolt under the table. Had someone kicked him? Mel? She'd not done that in a long time, not since they were kids. She'd tell him afterward that she was trying to get him to not say something that would get him in trouble or stir up problems. How could she know what he was going to say? That made no sense. But she insisted that she could tell. Over the years he'd found that sometimes it was just easier to go with it. After all, she had kept him out of trouble some of the time.

She was scowling at him now. When he looked at her, she shook her head, staring at him with lowered eyebrows. She reached for the bowl of roasted baby potatoes, saying, "These look lovely, Mom, thanks."

SHE FOLLOWED him downstairs after supper. "So, how's it going?"

Like she didn't know. Was this one of those

rhetorical questions she talked about, the ones people asked but you weren't supposed to answer?

"Okay, Jeff, tell me. I know how it all creeps up on you. I did for me and does for most students. How far behind are you?"

Why would she assume that he was behind? Did she have access to his classes? His computer? He looked at her suspiciously.

"Jeff?"

Why not start with the positive? "You were right. I thought I'd hate the Biology class that you forced me to take."

"I didn't *force* you to take it. I explained that you had to have at least one science class this term and gave you the list of possibilities. The bio class fit your schedule better than did some of the other options."

"It's really interesting, or at least the labs are. I'm doing so well in them that they offered me a job. I'm a lab assistant helping students work through their labs.

"Some of them are really not very good at this stuff. They seem to struggle with the lab lessons for some reason. Hard to understand when they're all online and everything is laid out well."

"Congratulations! That's cool getting a job. It will look good on your resume."

He talked a bit more about life in the lab, and then Mel asked about the Biology lectures.

Oh. Well. "They're not as good. Nothing hands-on, you're supposed to sit there and listen. Sometimes he shows pictures or a short movie clip, but mostly he just talks. I don't know how he can make it boring when the actual work in the lab is interesting."

"What about the textbook?"

"The lab book's all online. It's easy to access and full of examples and ways that this applies to real life."

"And the text that follows the lectures?"

"How did you know there was another textbook?"

She just looked at him.

"Well, I didn't. Agnes who runs the lab mentioned it to me. I hadn't realized there was a different book we're supposed to be reading. She says that a lot of the questions for the midterm will come from it. That's weird, don't you think, especially when it would make more sense to give us questions from the lab. We're only in lectures less than two-and-a-half hours a week, but most students spend at least double that amount of time on the labs."

"That's just the way it works." She picked up a book from the pile on the floor. "Philosophy Ethics. How's that class going?"

He smiled at his sister. "You were right again. It's another class I thought would be useless, but it's not. You need a moral compass to guide you."

Mel looked at him in disbelief.

"I didn't make that up; that's what the prof said the first day of classes." He remembered that well. It helped stick in his mind because it was only one of a handful of lectures he'd attended. He had read the textbook, though. Well, looked at it a couple of times.

Mel flipped through the book, noting that there was

some highlighting in chapters one and two. "Is this as far as you've gotten?"

He nodded.

"Oh, Jeff. It's almost midterm time. That means that you should be about halfway through the text by now."

"I doubt that. There's not been enough time. Look, I'll show you." He pulled up the course site. This was a reasonable instructor. He put all his lecture notes online so you could access them at any time. "I've been following along."

Mel nudged his hand away from the mouse and scrolled through the site. "There." She touched the monitor.

Jeff hated fingerprints on his screen. He pulled his sleeve over his hand and wiped away the offending smear.

"Sorry." She pointed without touching this time. "See? He gives a reading schedule to help you keep on track. By this week you should have completed chapter eleven." She looked at him. "Have you?"

"I got behind in some stuff."

Mel put her head back and let out a sigh. Then she took a big breath in. "Okay. It's still recoverable. This is just one subject. We'll work out a reasonable schedule to get you caught back up with your readings." From her bag she pulled out a pad of paper and pen. She knew that Jeff didn't like anyone touching his stuff. She wrote down the readings that needed to be done for this Philosophy class. "It's doable," she said.

She started to point to the screen but stopped herself just shy of touching it. "Pull up Biology, will ya? We need to see where you should be at with your readings for that class."

Jeff began telling her about how he was so far ahead in the Bio lab work that the program would not let him do anymore until after the midterms were over. She wasn't as impressed as he thought she should be.

"No assignments for that class? No. Good, then. What else are you taking?"

SHE MADE him go over it all, class by class, assignment by assignment, text readings and exams schedules included. It was a lot. An awful lot.

How could they expect students to do this much work? How could anyone keep up?

Mel said that it was possible, that lots of students managed it and that he could, too.

Huh! What did she know?

She said that the amount of time was not the issue, but how he spent his time caused him problems.

"A guy can't work every minute of the day or he'd go bonkers. I need some down time." What did Mel think he was?

Mel agreed, even pointing out that Jeff might need more down time than did some people. But that made it even more important for him to manage his time well.

"It's not as bad as I thought it might be," Mel said.

Gee, thanks, sis. Was that a vote of confidence? Or another criticism? It was sometimes hard to know with

Mel. Another of those annoying instances where people did not clearly state what they meant.

Mel helped Jeff make a schedule - a schedule that would start to get him back on track. She emphasized "start", saying that he could not possibly get caught up enough this weekend.

He knew that. "Then why didn't you come over earlier this week to give me a hand?" Wouldn't that have been more helpful rather than forcing him to try and cram all this stuff into just a few days?

Mel's voice got *that* tone, the one where she sometimes meant the opposite of what her words said. "I tried. What do you think all those messages I left you were about? I started last weekend as soon as I heard that you were home."

"Well, if you'd told me that's what the messages were about, we could have done something about this."

"Did you read any one them?"

"I started to, but there were so many of them. It would have taken hours for me to go through each one and reply to them all. I had stuff to do."

Mel's eyes glared at her eyebrows. She's perfected that expression in her teen years and never got over it.

Jeff stared at the written schedule his sister had created for him, which included the exact times of each day when he should be either reading a certain textbook or working on an assignment. She'd said that these were all estimates, their best guesses as to how long things might take. If he finished one thing early, she thought he should move right on to the next one. When he complained about the sheer volume of the stuff to be done, she pointed out that she'd built breaks into the schedule and that he would not be in this mess if he'd used a schedule and paid attention to due dates and syllabi earlier on.

AT THE TIME he could be ticked with Mel. She was (again) pointing out his shortcomings, being both helpful and critical at the same time. He grumbled at her bossy ways but listened because she just might be right. She made it seem doable - a lot of work, but possible.

Now, looking at the overwhelming workload, it seemed far, far from doable. As in what person could ever get all this stuff done?

Was it even worth trying? What if he made the effort, what if he exhausted himself, ignoring everything else and still didn't get it done? What if his best try wasn't good enough?

There were lots of instances in his life when his best had not been good enough. Take high school. No matter how much he'd try to rest up over the weekend, tried to brace himself for Monday, he'd still be taken unawares by the bullies who delighted in plaguing him. He'd tried to fit in, blend in, or whatever else his mother called it. He just wasn't a blending kind of guy.

Or, was he? It just occurred to him that while at college, he'd stopped looking over his shoulder, waiting for some trick to be played on him, for the laughter that would follow as he dropped his books or banged into the lockers from a shove from behind. Did that mean that he blended in? Finally? Or was it that the students from his high school were just not around on that campus?

Even if that problem was no longer the one that dominated his life, there were other things.

In high school, he had held onto the belief that he was smart. His marks were better than those of many other students, even students who tried hard. Jeff's marks were not consistently high - it depended on if the subject or assignment interested him. They gave a lot of dumb assignments in high school, ones not worth bothering about.

This made him think of some assignments he'd looked at in his college classes. He'd focused on the requirements that seemed interesting or important, ignoring the dumb ones. Mel pointed out that it didn't really matter if he felt them important, what mattered was that the prof believed they needed to be done and the prof got to make the rules.

Mel had added up his grades so far in each class. It wasn't pretty. She's averaged them to out of a hundred so that he could compare how he was doing in each class, then use that as a gauge to see where he should focus his efforts. Of course, his Biology mark was stellar, mainly because of his excellent lab work and because there were no assignments or tests yet for the lecture part.

But this was not the case in some of the other classes. Most, in fact.

Your marks reflected how smart you were. Those words echoed in Jeff's head.

While Mel said that this was not necessarily true, to Jeff it was. What other evidence was there? And, if you judged by how he was doing so far in college, he was not clever at all.

Maybe he wasn't. Maybe he had no business being in college. It was for other people, not ones like him who got distracted, who went into their own head, letting the world drop away while he did what interested him. Mel said the trick was to find a way to make those things meld, to find a way to turn the things he was passionate about into a career. She believed that college was a steppingstone to making that happen.

For her, perhaps, but obviously not for a guy like him.

CHAPTER 15

*O*ff to the gym.

Hard to believe that he was doing this voluntarily now. Yeah, it had taken tons of nagging from Mel to get him in the habit of working out. How could this be something he loved to hate? Or hated to love? It was the weirdest thing - he hated to go to the gym. That meant stopping what he was doing, which was most likely something much more fascinating on his computer. It meant leaving the house. It meant changing clothes.

Exercise made little sense to Jeff, but Mel insisted. She said it fell into the category of those things that might not make sense to Jeff but had to be done anyway. It was etiquette. It was protocol, part of those unwritten rules that everyone but him seemed to just know. Well, Mel rarely steered him wrong about such things and sometimes her guidance even helped.

Take this whole gym thing. His first reaction was, "Are you out of your mind?" Firmly in Jeff's head was the torture of gym class in high school where he was tormented by the jocks. Never coordinated, never catching on to team sports, never liking the possibility of physical contact, the gym and physical activity shrouded some of his worst memories. The noise, echoes and odors piled on the stress to levels he could not tolerate. How could anyone?

When he could take absolutely not one more minute of being inside a school, he quit. There was no way anyone on this planet was getting him to enter those doorways ever again. Their mom agreed to let him home school. Mel had said, "Huh" in that skeptical way she had of infusing all sorts of unidentified meaning into a single syllable.

She tried to tell him that all bodies needed physical activity. He knew she was wrong and that *his* body was much better off far removed from anything gym related.

But Mel had this way of wearing people down. And she thought *he* was annoying. Huh! See, he could do that word justice, too.

A year ago, she nagged the life out of Jeff and finally got him to come to the gym with her. Just once was the promise - to see what he thought of it. He could tell her his opinion on it without stepping foot inside the stinky place, but to get his sister off his back, he agreed to go. Once and once only.

THE PLACE MEL chose made little sense. The gym was called The Four Horsemen. Jeff looked it up online. What he found fit with his experience of gym class. Apocryphal, like the end of times. Your worst nightmare comes true.

Pestilence. Students in the gym had varying degrees of acne and skin eruptions. And the locker room stank like the Armageddon had come true.

War. The gymnasium and change rooms were like war zones. You never knew when you'd be attacked. Your body was not safe. Your mind was not safe. The hypervigilance was exhausting.

Death. He always felt that his body, let alone his mind, was in serious peril when he entered gym class. How many times had he been punched, pushed, tripped, shoved, and made fun of during those torture periods?

Famine. He starved on gym days in school. That final year when he endured as much as he could possibly take, gym class was right before lunch. When his clothes were taken from him, he couldn't get changed to go to the cafeteria. Sometimes they hid his things and it would take the whole lunch period before he could find his stuff. Even if he did, he was far too upset to be able to ingest any nourishment or keep it down. He needed to find a spot alone to breathe, to regroup, to try to get his head together.

So, Mel chose a gym called The Four Horsemen. Apt, in a way.

THE FIRST TIME HE WENT, he turned around after entering the doors. His ears were bombarded with music playing at decibels dangerous to any ear drum. But Mel was there and grabbed him by the arm. Sheesh. She knew he didn't like to be touched, even more so when he was upset. But she wouldn't let go. With her other hand palm out and face down, she made motions like she was dribbling a ball. Miraculously, the music went almost quiet.

"I arranged that they'd lower the music when you got here," she explained. Phew. Now that the noise wasn't assaulting his brain, he could take a look around. Rather than a mob of moving bodies like in gym class, there were only three other people in the building, at least that he could see. They weren't approaching him or looking at him from the corner of their eye. No one looked like they were planning anything against him; in fact, they seemed to pay no attention to him whatsoever. Hah. He'd been fooled by that before. But with only a few of them to be wary of, it might not be too hard to keep safe.

Oh, no. A guy was approaching. Jeff had tensed, ready for the attack. The guy stopped in front of them and held out his hand. "Hi, I'm Timothy. Would you like me to show you around?"

Was that code for trying to get him into the change room to dunk his head in the toilet? But no, Mel knew about all that old stuff and she was smiling at Tim. "Tim's my trainer," she explained, "and he'll help you, too."

Trainer? Who said anything about training? He was just here to look around to get his sister off his back.

As he stood frozen, Mel gave him that look, that sister look he knew only too well. If he didn't cooperate with her, he would never hear the end of it. With a sigh, he shook Tim's hand.

"Come on this way," the guy said. "Is there anything in particular you want to work on?"

Work on? "No, I'm just here because my sister thought I should take a look".

"Fair enough. I'll show you what we have to offer."

They went on a tour of the equipment. Some were intriguing. He appreciated the engineering that went into the smooth glide and resistance mechanisms of some of the machines.

"Wanna try that one out?" Timothy asked.

Jeff glanced at Mel. This wasn't part of the plan, but she was always telling him that it was okay to go with the flow sometimes. She'd explained that it was all right to do something even if it was not in the original plan.

He was a geek in some ways but not necessarily in mechanical things. In gym class, he'd never really been sure of the rules and game plays. Would this be the same way?

"I'll show you how this works."

Good. Jeff was a visual learner and would get more from a demonstration than a verbal explanation. Okay. It made sense and Jeff liked the analytical way that Tim broke down the muscle group targeted by each piece of equipment.

There was no one else lining up to use the machines.

No pushing or shoving. In fact, no one except for Tim seemed to be paying him any attention. Even Mel had gone off to do her own thing, with her earbuds in place.

"Do you want to work here for a while, or would you prefer that I show you everything first?"

So, Tim understood that there were different ways of learning. Jeff looked at the trainer closely. No, this didn't seem to be a trick question with a right or wrong answer. He was just asking. Good. A guy you could take at face value. Refreshing. Maybe this gym thing wouldn't be so bad.

"A lot of our clients prefer to bring their own music and headphones or ear buds. They sort of get lost in their own worlds while working out." Better and better, Jeff could relate to this.

So, he tried it and it wasn't so bad. That Tim guy interrupted him a couple of times, telling him to go easy on this, it being his first time and to switch it up on different machines using different muscle groups so that he wouldn't be too sore later.

For the first while, Jeff kept a wary eye on the door, checking to see who came in and what they might do or say to him. But everyone ignored him, apart from a nod or quick hi when they went by. No idle chit chat, no mocking. No competition. Tim explained that here people competed against themselves to work on improving their fitness level.

While physical exercise had never been his thing, Jeff

had to admit that, once he got into it, there were benefits. He liked the way his body felt tired, but in a good way. It felt used, in a way that it was supposed to.

So, he continued. Mel went twice a week and Jeff went with her. Then he upped it to three or four times a week because he liked the way it made him feel.

There were days when he didn't want to go, when it was an effort to stop what he was doing and prepare himself to leave the house.

Mel had rules around this. She said that he had to shower before coming - maybe not right before, but at least that day. Now, did that make any sense? He was only going to get all sweated up at the gym and need to shower again. She also said that he needed to change his clothes before coming to the gym, so it didn't look like he was wearing what he'd slept in. Why would anyone care? His sleeping clothes looked remarkably like what he wore in the day anyway.

On gym days he changed his clothes several times - once before leaving for the gym and again after working out. It meant two showers as well - one before leaving home and another at the gym after exercising. How did that make sense?

That part he had resisted. Strongly. Images flooded his mind with the torture he'd endured in the high school locker room, the terror of what would be done to him in the showers, the fear of never knowing if his clothes would be gone and he'd have nothing but a towel to wear to the next class.

Trusting his sister, he'd agreed to try a shower at the Four Horsemen, leery that it would indeed turn out apocryphal for him. But he was alone in the change room the entire time. Mel had checked with Tim about the times of day when there would be few people around and Jeff stuck pretty much to those times, even if Mel couldn't make it some days.

Once, while in the shower, Jeff froze. Over the fall of soft water from the rain shower faucet, he heard the door to the change room bang shut. Then there was the metallic sound of a locker opening and a gym bag hitting the ground. Jeff stood under the flow, paralyzed with what might come next. Scene after scene from high school played in his mind, each more horrifying and humiliating than the last.

Then the change room door clanged again, and all was silent. When his heart slowed to a safer level, Jeff shut off the water and listened. Silence. With all the caution born of hard-won experience, Jeff wrapped his waist with a towel, then opened the shower door. Still silence. Slightly bolder, he moved through the area but not a soul was around. That is, if you didn't count a gym bag thrown on the floor with some of its contents spilling out. Didn't that guy know what the school bullies might do if you left your stuff laying around like that? Maybe he didn't care, knew that they wouldn't dare touch his things.

Jeff made his way to his locker, taking a deep breath before looking inside. His clothes were all there, just as he'd left them. His shoulders relaxed and his jaw unclenched. Mel just might be right, and this place had nothing in common with high school gym class.

While home for reading week, he might as well visit the gym. Although getting ready to go there was a drag, he always felt better after working out. Somehow, he'd forgotten that and never thought to find a gym at college.

As he walked to The Four Horsemen, Jeff's thoughts were on the comparisons and the sets he planned to increase today. He'd been gradually getting his reps up and was proud of his progress. It seemed a little archaic that the gym provided clients with a paper and pencil way to keep track of their progress, but Mel said, "When in Rome…". As if *that* made any kind of sense. They were clearly not in Rome, not even in Italy for that matter. But she explained that when you were somewhere, it made sense to fall in with the customs of that place. Although it would be much more efficient to do things electronically, Jeff complied and at the start of each visit, picked up his sheet from the front desk. Only he and Tim seemed to glance at it and there were no comments about his progress or lack thereof.

Jeff was so engrossed with these thoughts that it didn't register that a voice was calling to him. Not just *a* voice, but several of them. Deep voices, so it wasn't Mel.

His heart lurched. It had been years since he had heard those voices singing out his name, but oh, did he remember them. His nemesis. The worst of the gym class tormentors.

"Jeffrey! Hey, Jeffrey, old man. How's it hangin'?"

Maybe if I just keep on going, they'll ignore me.

Fat chance. As if that had ever worked.

Glancing around, Jeff wondered if he should cross the road. That way he wouldn't have to run into these guys. Would they cross as well?

As if reading his mind, Robert, the biggest (and meanest, in Jeff's opinion), stepped into the street at an angle. Robert had been a running back on the high school football team and Jeff knew that he'd never outrun him. The guys with him were Trevor and Blake - the trifecta of who Jeff never wanted to see again in his life. He braced himself for what he knew would come.

"Hey Jeffie. Is that you, old man?" Robert nudged Blake. "Look at little Jeffie, all grown up."

Blake laughed. "Whatcha been up to, Jeffie? Did you ever finish high school?" He pretended to frown and think. "Oh, that's right. You dropped out, didn't you?"

Jeff remained rooted to where he was. All those old feelings coursed through him. The taunts, the names, being pushed around, being made to feel the biggest looser to ever walk the halls of that hated school.

Trevor looked uncomfortable. "Come on, guys. Leave him alone. This isn't high school anymore."

"What? I'm just asking after an old classmate." Turning back to Jeff, he asked, "So, what happened? Are you headed back to grade eleven to try again?"

Jeff weighed his options. Back in school he'd tried it both ways - responding to their taunts and keeping silent. Neither worked in his favor. "I'm on my way to the gym."

Robert and Blake hooted. "The gym! We had some

fine old times in the gym, didn't we? Remember that time we gave you a swirly? Or when…"

"Guys knock it off," said Trevor. "Leave him alone. You were jerks back then; no need to be jerks now."

Jeff looked at Trevor. While Trevor had never actually taken part in any of the physical stuff against him in school, he'd been part of the group that Blake and Robert hung out with. You know, the jock set. The pick-on-the-loner-type. Maybe Trevor hadn't instigated stuff, but he sure didn't stop it, either.

Blake and Robert advanced. Jeff knew all too well just how inventive these guys could be. Even though he was a grown-assed man now, all the feelings of inadequacy, of fear, of loneliness from his teen years flooded back in, overwhelming him. He froze.

Fight, flight or freeze. His brain chose freeze, just like it always had. How had that worked for him?

He was no longer surrounded by jeering teenage boys or cramped in washroom or between open locker doors. He was on a street with yards of area around him.

"What's your hurry, Jeffie?" This came from Robert. "Why not stay a while and shoot the shit with us? You know, catch up on old times?' He grinned at Blake "I remember some of those times, don't you?" He advanced.

Blake came at him from the other side; this was a maneuver he and Robert had used over and over during their high school bullying days.

Jeff knew it all too well. He stepped to the right, one foot on the curb, the other on the road. He held up his hands. "Enough, guys. We're not kids anymore. Just go." Further words failed him as they did when his anxiety soared. He'd never had the words to ward off these tormentors; he never would.

Then he made an error, one he never would have made back in high school. He took his eyes off one of them. While he watched Blake's approach, he forgot to watch out for Robert. How many times had he been caught like that? It was years ago, and he must be rusty.

Blake sped up his approach. Jeff backed up, already slightly off balance with one foot off the curb, six inches lower than the other. As he took another step backwards, he didn't notice Robert down on one knee behind him, perfectly positioned. Robert and Blake had honed this tactic over the years, although they had not practiced in quite some time.

Jeff's next step back knocked him over Robert's knee. With the help of Robert's left elbow, Jeff fell backwards into the street.

Robert scrambled to his feet. "Geez, Jeffie. Watch where you're going why doncha? You plowed right into me." His satisfied grin was nasty to behold.

"You ass." Jeff waited for Trevor to continue, to join in with the litany of what a loser he was.

"Aren't you guys ever going to grow up? I don't know why I'm hanging around with you." Trevor turned to Jeff and held out his hand. "Sorry about these guys. Obviously, they still act like high school kids."

Jeff looked at Trevor's hand. He was not taken in. It had happened before, someone offering to give him a hand up only to drop him or shove him or do something else to humiliate him.

"Come on. I'm not like those jack-asses." Trevor looked at Jeff.

Jeff's mind raced. While in a state of panic it had not always registered just who it was doing what to him during those torture sessions in high school. Yeah, Trevor had been on the periphery, but had he actually done anything? Said anything? Hard to say.

Well, he was not a kid anymore. He didn't care what these guys nor anyone else thought of him. There wasn't a whole hallway full of kids ready to laugh and jeer at his humiliation. So, what if he took the offer of Trevor's hand up and Trevor let him go. No one but these idiots were around, other than the odd vehicle that might pass by. Likely things would not get any more out of hand than this.

Jeff reached up his right hand. The two men locked palms around each other's wrists and Trevor pulled. Jeff came to his feet more nimbly than he would have a year ago. Yeah, the gym work was paying off. Trevor released Jeff's arm. "Sorry about these idiots. You'd think they'd grow up, wouldn't you?"

"Arrested development, I believe it's called."

The three looked at him.

"That's what they called it in my psychology class. Stunts your mental and emotional growth."

Robert glared. Blake looked like he wasn't sure he got it.

Trevor laughed. He fell in beside Jeff. "Where'd you say you were going? Some gym?"

"Yeah, The Four Horsemen." He kept walking.

"What's with that name? I think I've heard that somewhere before. Like maybe in English class? The Bible?"

"It's from the Bible, but I think it's mentioned other places as well. I have no idea why they'd call a gym something like that, but the place is okay."

"I've not worked out since I quit football after grade twelve". He patted his gut. "It shows, doesn't it?"

Jeff took a quick glance at his old classmate's midriff. He wasn't used to checking out guys or really paying that much attention to anyone's physical appearance. "Yeah, it does."

There was a pause before Trevor laughed again. "You haven't changed. Still a straight-up guy. That's not a bad thing."

They walked on in silence. Jeff glanced behind but didn't see Robert and Blake following them.

"Never mind those guys. Forget them. They're idiots." Then, more to himself said, "I don't know why I'm hanging out with them."

"Why do you?" Jeff had never understood some people's need to simply be around others, even when they didn't particularly like them.

"I guess we see each other at work and have known each other for years, so it just sort of happens."

"Where do you work?" Mel would be pleased at how Jeff was asking questions to keep the conversation going.

"Walmart."

Walmart? Whoa. That place was creepy. Who could

stand going there, let alone work there day after day? The place overwhelmed the senses with the lights and colors and noise and people.

The lights. Who needed lights glaring into your eyes with such intensity? Sunglasses should be given out at the door if they didn't want to blind their customers. Or, maybe that was it – it was a ploy to get shoppers to buy sunglasses there.

The crowds. There were so many people there. Always. People talking, kids yelling, people laughing. They'd stop abruptly, block the aisles and never give a thought to whomever they might brush against.

The noise. The squeaking carts. Have they never heard of oil? The incessant beeps at the checkout counters. The public address system screaming announcements at holy decibels. Human ears were not meant to withstand such torture. It was enough to make every hair on your body take notice, stand at attention then try to peel off of your body, or so it felt.

No, just no. Why would anyone choose to go inside such a building? How could these guys be reduced to working in such a place?

Trevor watched Jeff's face and tried to guess his thoughts.

"I know. It's not what I imagined for myself after high school. I thought I was ready to take on the world. We were riding high after that last football trophy. But then we found out that in the real world, playing football didn't really matter unless you were good enough for the pros. I wasn't. None of us were.

"You can't freeload off your parents forever, so I

needed a job. Blake was already stocking shelves at Walmart, so I applied, too. Seems like they always want workers, so I got hired, then Robert did. But our hours aren't full-time, just casual, so none of us make that much, not enough for our own places. So, we share an apartment."

These were the jocks, the rulers of the school, thought Jeff. These guys strutted around like they owned the place and look where they ended up. "Walmart?"

"Yeah, it's pretty bad. It's just temporary, though, until I find something better."

"At least you make money."

"Not much - a couple bucks above minimum wage."

"How long have you been there?"

"Three years."

Silence.

"It's not so bad," Trevor continued. We work a lot of night or late shifts so it's quiet. It's worse in the day because customers keep coming up to ya and asking where stuff is. Mostly we try to hide if we see someone coming.

"And there are other guys there. We get together for LAN parties; most of us play the same video games. And we watch for the sales so we can bring home cheap pizzas and snacks."

He watched Jeff out of the corner of his eyes. "So, what about you? What are you up to?"

"I'm going to the gym."

"I mean apart from that?"

"I'm home for a week on break from college."

"Oh yeah? I always meant to go to college. What's it like?"

What's it like. Good question. "Okay, I guess. Some subjects I don't like, and some are better than I thought they'd be. You're mostly left on your own, which is good. It's a lot of work, though."

"But you're smart. It would be easier for you."

Smart? Me? He thinks I'm smart? Everyone thought I was such a dork at school, a dumb dork.

Trevor continued. "I thought I wanted to go to college, too. Make something of myself. I don't think I have what it takes, though." He walked a bit farther. "It sucks stocking shelves. Mindless. Can't see myself doing this for the rest of my life."

"Why don't you apply for college? It's not that hard. My sister helped me pick classes and stuff. She'd probably help you too if you asked."

"Yeah? Nah, I don't think it's for me, but I'll think about it. Thanks."

CHAPTER 16

*H*ome. He was free to get lost in his computer, explore and code and work on projects all he wanted. Or play video games. Day, night, and hours lost meaning because he was on his own agenda, on his own terms.

Even the living part was easy. Mom provided meals. Sure, she called him when lunch and supper were ready, but if he was busy or sleeping, no problem. She would make him something when he got hungry. Stuff like laundry was easy, too. His mom would gather up stuff that was on his floor and throw the clothes in the wash. They'd be returned clean, folded and sometimes, if she knew where they belonged, even put away in drawers. That latter had pros and cons though - nice to not have to give clothing on the floor the sniff test to see if they could be worn again, but with things being put in drawers, it made it hard to find them.

And, he was alone. Phil was not a bad guy, but when

you're used to having a large room to yourself, sharing crimped your style. Even when he was quiet, he was *there*. And Jeff had to keep remembering not to hog the whole room.

Sometimes it was nice to have a roommate to talk to or to go to lunch with. They even helped each other occasionally with course work, but mostly Jeff was used to being a solitary creature.

MOM WAS PRETTY big on this whole college idea before he went. But now she seemed to have changed her mind. She kept saying that it was all right for him to stay home if that's what he wanted.

Why? Was she lonely? Jeff had heard about empty-nest syndrome. Did she miss him too much? Was it his job to give her a purpose, something to do with her life? Did she miss having a kid to look after?

LOOK AFTER. Is that what he was? A kid? Someone who needed looking after? Is that how he wanted to be thought of? Jeff had never paid much attention to how people regarded him, but after meeting his former classmates yesterday, it was on his mind.

Those guys were the cream of the students at their high school, or at least that's how they acted. They were the ones everyone looked up to, the ones who had it all together, the ones kids wanted to be like.

Did Jeff want to be like them? Not now, that's for sure.

Walmart. Who would have guessed? The most promising students from the football team were lowly clerks at a department store. They had not even risen in their positions for the last three years. Jeff could not imagine doing the same thing now that he'd been doing for several years.

Correction. He *could* see himself doing the same thing if that thing involved doing stuff on his computer. But that was on his own terms and stuff of his choosing that interested him or made him some money when he took on short coding projects.

Putting cans on shelves? Answering the call for "clean-up on aisle fourteen"? Directing old ladies to the washroom or the toilet paper section? Geez. How could they stand it?

And the three of them lived together. Jeff found it hard to live with one other guy, let alone two.

Way back in high school, those guys used to be big gamers. Sounded like they still were. Nothing wrong with that.

JEFF REMEMBERED Mel coming downstairs to see him last summer.

She'd asked, "Where are you going with your life?"

That made so little sense. Going? He wasn't going anywhere, obviously. He was sitting in his office chair, in front of his computer. The chair might be on rollers (high quality ones, too), but he wasn't going anywhere, he told her.

"Exactly," she said.

He wished that she would use plain English and just say what she meant.

"You need to have a plan. What you're doing right this minute may not be how you want your life to look in five or ten years."

Who could plan that far ahead?

"It's fine to live with mom and dad right now but they won't be here forever."

Wasn't that a bit morbid? Sure, everyone dies sometime and yeah, they were old, but not that old.

"Mom won't always be able to look after you."

I can look after myself, he thought.

"It's all those little things she does for you. You know, like take care of all your daily necessities like food and dishes and cleaning and paying the bills."

"She likes to cook for me. She says so. And she doesn't want anyone else messing up her kitchen."

"True, mom is protective of her kitchen. But don't you feel bad relying so heavily on her?"

He'd never given it any thought. She was just there, and she did stuff. "I've never heard her complain."

"You wouldn't. For one thing, you're rarely upstairs enough to hear her and for another, she feels that she has to do it because you're unable to manage for yourself."

What! Where would she get an idea like that?

"Think about what she does. Take lunch for

example. She sets the table. She makes the food and serves it. Afterward she clears the table, puts the leftovers away, does the dishes and tidies the kitchen. She goes to sit in the living room then you come upstairs asking what's to eat and she has to begin all over again."

Jeff hadn't thought of it that way. He ate when he was hungry. He'd get so involved in his computer that he didn't hear anyone call him for lunch.

Mom didn't like anyone messing in her kitchen and that applied more so to Jeff. She said that he left the place a disaster and it was easier for her to get the food ready herself. So, Jeff let her. If that's what she said, she must mean it.

Mel wouldn't let it go. "Instead of making and cleaning up after three meals a day, it's more like six meals when you need yours prepared separately.

"I never asked her to do all that."

"True, but it works out that way."

"Do you think I should move out?"

"No. Maybe. At some time for sure, but not necessarily right now. I'd like you to think about what you want out of life and go for it, rather than just drifting and letting the years go by. Make a plan. Work toward it. Try things. See some of life that's outside these basement walls."

"I like these walls."

"You *think* you do, but maybe it's just what you've become used to. It feels safe and known. There might be things you'd enjoy more."

Then she'd talked about what he might learn at college and got his interest up. She'd been right and it had been okay, parts of it more than okay.

But...

What kind of a loser screwed up in his classes? Well, not all his classes. He aced Biology and even got a paying job out of it. (A job that paid more an hour than those guys made at Walmart after being there three years).

What kind of a loser stocked shelves year after year? It was a job and jobs paid the bills. But to do that same thing year in and year out, after bragging about all the things they were going to do after high school? How did that make sense?

Speaking of losers, what kind of loser was *he*?

While it was comfortable back in this basement, three years from now would he still be here, doing exactly the same thing? And, would that be so bad?

One of the plugs Mel made for college is that it would open his mind to different things. At the time he could not imagine that there would be anything outside of his computer that he would want to learn or experience. Really, through it, he had access to the world, didn't he?

But she'd been right about Biology. If he'd stayed at

home, he never would have explored that subject. The Ethics course had points that he'd not considered. Mel said that college would get him out of his own head. Maybe she was right.

Well, he'd tried it. He'd been there for a whole six weeks. They weren't a bad six weeks overall, although some parts definitely sucked.

How would he feel if he never went back? Mom said that he didn't have to, and she seemed happy to have him back at home. What would that say about him if he tried college for just half of one semester then quit? Did he care what anyone thought? Not really, but he might care about what he thought of himself.

There had been a change; something changed in him during this time away. He saw himself differently. He wasn't just this computer geek who holed up in his parents' basement. He was an adult on campus, doing what thousands of these other students did. And, better than some of them did, judging by the students he helped in the Bio lab.

If he quit now, would he ever go back? From experience, Jeff knew how things worked in his mind, how the bad things were fretted upon, and seemed to multiply until he'd do almost anything to avoid them. Would school be like that for him? Did it matter?

He was comfortable at home. He made all the money he needed with the online contracts he picked up here and there. But, like Mel said, was that enough? Would there come a time when he wanted more - to do more, to be more?

Losers got stuck stocking shelves. Did losers also get stuck living in their parents' basements?

But look at the mess he was in. He was so far behind. Was there a way out of this?

He took off his headphones and opened the Messenger app on his phone. "Mel…"

CHAPTER 17

"Hey!"

Phil looked up. "Hey. Glad you're back. The way you left I wasn't sure if you would be."

"Yeah, for a while there I wasn't sure either."

"Things were quiet this week while you were gone. Not many students around. When I got bored, I went for a walk around some parts of the campus I'd never checked out before. You know how you get so wrapped up in your classes and are just trying to tread water."

Jeff puzzled about the treading water bit, but Phil continued.

"I found this gym. Really just a small thing in the basement of the Physics building. It's not like a gymnasium where you'd play sports but an exercise room with machines.

"I didn't really know how to use them but since

there wasn't anyone around, I thought I'd try some out. It was okay until this girl walked in. I felt like an idiot, sure I was doing it all wrong. I didn't think she was going to come in when she saw me, but then she did anyways. And she asked me how you were supposed to use that machine. She'd tried but didn't get the hang of it.

"Ah, that's where you come in."

"Me? I wasn't even around."

"Well, I sort of talked about you. I told her that my roommate worked out all the time and went to a gym back home, so he'd know all about how to run this equipment."

Jeff's eyebrows rose. "Me?"

"Yeah. I kind of used you. I told her that when you get back, you'd probably be willing to show her." His cheeks reddened. "Was that okay? Would you? I mean, would you mind showing her? And me?"

Jeff reflected. This had been an interesting week of revelations. "Okay."

"Great!" Phil got up and headed for the door. "Let's go. Coming?"

"I guess we could do that now. But how do you know she's there?"

Phil colored again. "I don't. I'm hoping she won't be and that you can show me some of the stuff so that I don't look like such a dweeb the next time I meet her there."

∼

"This girl. Is she a Physics major?"

"No. Why'd you guess that?"

"She was in the Physics building."

"Oh, yeah. Makes sense. No, she's a music major. She said she was feeling stressed from all the assignments she had due, went for a walk to clear her head and found the gym a few days ago." They were almost at there. "*Her* parents don't think music is a useless pastime. They're both into it themselves."

Jeff and Phil were taking turns spotting each other and counting reps. The sweat poured off Phil as he tried to push the weights that Jeff made look almost effortless. "Don't worry. That was how I was a year ago, but it doesn't take long before you build muscles and it's easier," Jeff assured him.

"I sure hope that's true," said a voice from behind them. "Hi, Phil," she continued.

Grabbing a towel, Phil wiped off his face and neck. "Geez, I'm a mess. Sorry." He sprayed down the seat he'd been on and rubbed it dry, trying to compose himself. "Alanna, this is my roommate, Jeff Nicols. Jeff, this is Alanna, the girl I was telling you about."

The door opened and another woman entered. "Hi, Trish. I just got here. This is Phil and Jeff. Guys, my friend, Trish." Turning to Trish, she said, "This is the guy Phil was telling me about, the one who can show us how to use all these machines."

It wasn't all that different than instructing students in the Biology lab. It took all of Jeff's time explaining and helping the four of them, adjusting the weight and tension levels to what he thought appropriate for each. The girls weren't very strong, Trish in particular. She tired out quickly as well.

"I think I've had enough for today. Thanks for showing us. I'm sure we're safer around this stuff now."

Jeff was quite sure that was true.

"After we get cleaned up, Alanna and I were heading to the cafeteria for a quick bite, and then going to the early show. It's a really old one, *Casablanca*. I love those oldies. Do you guys wanna join us?"

It wasn't really a date or anything, more like a bunch of friends hanging out. Still it had been years since Jeff had done anything like this. It was nice, especially when they agreed to meet for lunch the next day as well.

The work didn't go away.

Well, some of it had. With Mel's help, Jeff took another look at his classes and what he could reasonably get caught up in. Some things were doable, but some not so much. She had explained about deadlines and dropping classes. It wasn't really like failing them, more like postponing them. If you withdrew before a certain date, you'd not get a failing grade. Sometimes it was better to withdraw and try it again later rather than getting a poor mark or spreading yourself so thin that all your marks suffered. Or so she explained it to him.

Jeff withdrew from Calculus. That was a good choice because it was offered again at summer school. The same with English. That one had so much reading attached to it that Jeff had not a hope of getting through it all in less than a week. He could pick up those two classes later.

Although it felt rather like failing, once the withdrawals were done, the burden on his shoulders lifted. What was left was manageable. He could do it and do it well.

It was still work, though.

PHIL REMOVED his headphones and stretched. He got up. "I'm going to the vending machine. Want anything?"

"Yeah, something salty, please." He pointed the collection of coins near the edge of his desk.

"Nah, I've got this one."

After the door closed, Jeff was distracted by the sounds escaping Phil's headphones; he'd not shut off his music before leaving. What was that? Jeff wheeled his chair closer to Phil's desk. Still couldn't hear it well enough. Reaching over, he picked up the headphones, holding one side to his ear. Neat stuff!

Then Phil was looming over him.

"Sorry, man." Jeff knew how much he hated anyone touching his things. He should not have grabbed Phil's. "It's just that I could hear this stuff coming from your headphones and it was like nothing I've heard."

"I know. I'm weird. I like different sorts of music."

"I like it. What is it?"

"It's an album called Cartographer by E. S. Posthumus. The E.S. stands for Experimental Sounds and Posthumus is about things past." When he saw that Jeff truly was interested, he unplugged his headset to let the music fill their room. Some of it is sung by Luna Sans and some of it has a choir and orchestra playing her parts." He was still defensive. "I know it's not the kind of music most people listen to."

"Here's what's on mine." Jeff unplugged his headphones to let Lindsey Stirling's violin work come out.

"Cool." They listened a few more minutes. "Would you mind not using your headphones for a while? I'd like to listen to it while I work, too."

Hesitantly, Jeff removed his headphones from around his neck. He *always* wore them when at his computer. They efficiently blocked out everything and everyone but what he wanted to focus on. A glance showed him that Phil was back at work, looking like he had no plans to interfere with what Jeff was doing. Slowly Jeff returned his hands to his keyboard. If he turned the music up just a bit, then he would not be able to hear the tiny clicks coming from Phil's keyboard. Yes, this could work. It was sort of companionable to both work away while listening to the same music.

AGNES SIGNALED to Jeff as soon as he entered the biology lab. "How's it going?"

"Okay." He was cautious. Agnes was aware of how things were going with Jeff in the lab. She could see his progress and that of the students he helped. What exactly was she asking?

"Have you made plans for the summer?"

This was just the end of March. Summer was a long way off. Didn't she know that he had enough to do right now without planning that far ahead?

"I mean, do you think you'll be sticking around campus during spring and summer sessions? This first year Biology course is not easy for some students and a number of them will be taking it over again or will try it for the first-time during May to August. We could use a good lab instructor."

"Yes, you could."

"I mean, do you have any interest in working here for spring and summer?"

Did he? It held some appeal. It was comfortable here and he was good at helping those students who seemed to struggle.

"Can I think about it?"

He mentioned it over lunch with Phil, Alanna, and Trish. They met up quite often these days and they'd sort of started to pair off. Not that Jeff had much to do with that, but gradually Trish had most often sat by him or walked beside him when the four of them went anywhere. She texted him several times a day, too. During one of their texting sessions, Jeff asked her if she wanted to go grab a coffee. Then they did it more often.

The first time Trish put her arm through his, Jeff pulled away. He was not used to being touched.

Trish blushed and mumbled, "Sorry."

Jeff took a deep breath and reached for her arm with his other hand. He looped it back through his. Without looking at her he tried to explain. "I have this thing called tactile sensitivities. It means that sometimes a light touch feels bad, like it makes me skin crawl."

Trish pulled her arm away.

"No! I don't mean you. I mean when I'm not expecting it. It just startled me, that's all." He gave her the smile his mom said would charm the bark off a log. "With you, I like it." Her arm stayed there.

When he held open the door for her, it seemed natural to reach for her hand as they continued down the hallway to the cafeteria.

THE PRESSURE WAS ON. Dropping two classes helped, but there was still a lot of work to finish before the term ended next week. He knew that anxiety would have shut him down if he'd been faced with completing the assignments for all five classes plus studying for the final exams. Mel was right. It was not just a matter of being smart enough, but organization and concentration mattered. He was better at attending to a few things well than spreading himself too thin. His grades had come up also now that he only worked on three classes at a time.

Mel had also told him that a big part of first year was learning how to do college. That hadn't made sense at first, but he got it now.

Back to work.

PHIL PUSHED BACK from his desk and stretched. He asked Jeff what he was listening to.

"Luka Sulic". He unplugged his headset so Phil could hear the cello music.

"If you like that kind of stuff, why aren't you taking music classes?"

"I don't want to *make* that music or need to know how it's done. I just like listening to it." He noticed Phil's silence. "What? You don't like it?" He plugged his headphones back in.

"No! I do. It's just that I don't just like listening, I like making music, too."

"I haven't heard you playing anything. Do you only do it when you go home?"

"No, I hardly do it there either."

That made no sense. "Why wouldn't you be doing what you like?"

"In my family, there are only certain things considered acceptable. Music isn't one of them."

"Are they part of some group that is anti-music?"

"No. My parents see music as frivolous. They're practical and believe that I need to go into something where I can make a living. Music isn't like that."

Jeff pointed to his computer. "These guys make a lot of money from their 2Cellos gigs."

"But it's not a sure thing, like getting a degree in business or engineering would be."

"It's not their life."

"Easy for you to say. You don't have to live with them. There's a lot of pressure on me to get what they call a 'proper' degree, one with a definite career attached."

"They can't make you."

"I know and they're not like that. But they're my folks. They've been good to me and they're paying for my tuition. They worry about me and don't want me to have to work in a factory like my dad does, even when he doesn't like it."

"But you might end up doing a job you don't like either."

A pause. "Yeah, I know." He replaced his headphones and his hand went to his mouse.

EPILOGUE

"Jeff, I was wondering," asked Phil. "Have you thought about what you want to do next year?"

Jeff looked up from his computer monitor.

"I mean about where you want to live."

"No." Who had time to think about such things?

Phil, obviously. "I've been thinking. It's been okay here, but it's pretty cramped, don't you think?"

It was. "I'd like more room to spread out my stuff, yeah."

"I went to look at options while you were at home that week. They have some accommodations that weren't available to us as first year students. They have these apartments. They're a bit further away but some have two bedrooms, a small living room, kitchen, and our own bathroom. You have the option of paying to eat in the cafeteria or cooking for yourself."

This had Jeff's attention.

"It costs more than a room like this does, but you

could save some money cooking for yourself." Phil warmed to the subject. "It would be nice to have a bathroom to ourselves, without having to share it with ten other guys."

Jeff had this thing about smells. Some were good, some neutral and some put him off. Badly. When you walked into the shower room here, you never knew which might assault your senses. It was so bad some days that Jeff could not stand to be in the room long enough to take a shower.

"Could we move now?"

Phil laughed. "Don't I wish. No, I'm talking about for next fall. Are you interested?"

"Yeah."

"We'd have to put in our application soon and put down a deposit." He looked away, then back again. "I think that we got along okay this year. Would you want to be roommates again next year? On the application there's a place to put the name of the person you'd prefer to room with. If you leave it blank, they will just assign anyone."

Was this what it felt like to have a friend? Someone who wanted to hang out with you? It had been over a decade since Jeff had had a buddy. "Where do we go sign up?"

As they waited in line at the Housing Office, something else occurred to Jeff. "You know, I'm thinking of coming to summer school. And spring session. That way I can catch up on the classes I dropped."

"Me, too."

"You didn't drop any classes, did you?"

"Nah, but I want to take some other things." His gaze narrowed. "I did what my parents wanted this year and took what they saw as 'sensible' classes and I did all right. Now I want to take what I want to take."

"Music?"

"Yeah. I've been looking and I can't get into the ones I really want until I first take the intro class, but then there's some pretty interesting stuff. I thought I'd do the intro class during spring session, then the good stuff during summer."

"So, you can take two classes then and two more in summer?"

"I'd like to finish my degree in three years rather than four, so I think I'll just keep going, as long as my money holds out."

"Me, too. My sister told me that I might do best when taking just one class at a time, getting in and out quick with no other distractions."

"Me, too." Phil stopped and turned around. "Let's go back to the Housing Office and apply to share an apartment during spring and summer sessions."

"Sure." It was nice to have a friend.

Thank you for spending your valuable time with this book. If you have enjoyed it the author would be greatly appreciative if you would leave a review on Amazon. Here is the link. Reviews mean a lot to authors and they are the way that new readers discover the work. (If you're not sure how to leave a review, contact the author at the link below and she'll be happy to show you how to do it.)

ENJOYED THIS BOOK?

Care for a **free book**? Click here to download your copy of the award-winning Amazon bestseller *Autism Goes to School*.

Author Dr. Sharon Mitchell loves connecting with readers. Contact her through her website at http://www.drsharonmitchell.org. There you will find information on her other books, her workshop appearances and questions families and teachers often ask about kids who have autism spectrum disorders.

Would you like to join the author's review team? Team members receive complimentary, advance copies of each new title. Contact Sharon at http://www.drsharonmitchell.org.

ABOUT THE AUTHOR

Dr. Sharon A. Mitchell has a Ph.D. in Psychology Management, specializing in autism spectrum disorders. Her Master's work looked at the long-term outlook for young people with Asperger's Syndrome and high functioning autism. Her career has been spent as a consultant, counsellor and special education teacher.

She has presented to thousands of participants in workshops and conferences. Her passion is helping those who are autistic and the people who support them.

She is also author of the books in the School Daze series, all available on your favorite online booksellers. You can also ask for them in libraries and bookstores.

When she is not writing, you'll find her farming, working on yard projects or welding.

You can reach Dr. Mitchell at questions@drsharonmitchell.org, at her website http://www.drsharonmitchell.org or on social media at these links:

Twitter - http://www.twitter.com/autismsite

Facebook - http://www.facebook.com/drsharonamitchell
Pinterest - https://www.pinterest.ca/mitchellsha3047/
Instagram - https://www.instagram.com/autismsite/
Website - http://www.drsharonmitchell.org/

- facebook.com/drsharonamitchell
- twitter.com/autismsite
- instagram.com/autismsite
- bookbub.com/authors/sharon-a-mitchell

OTHER BOOKS IN THE SERIES

There's more!

Care for a free book? Grab your copy of *Autism Goes to School*, the first novel in the series here.

You might also enjoy the other novels in the autism School Daze series. Each portrays a different child who has an autism spectrum disorder. Many of the same characters appear in each book.

Autism Goes to School
Autism Runs Away
Autism Belong
Autism Talks and Talks
Autism Grows Up
Autism Goes to College
Autism Box Set
#ad

Nonfiction books:

OTHER BOOKS IN THE SERIES

Autism Questions Parents Ask & the Answers They Need
Autism Questions Teachers Ask & the Answers They Need
#ad
As an Amazon Associate, I earn from qualifying purchases

Coming soon:

- The Autism Goes to School Workbook - Companion Workbook to Autism Goes to School
- Autism and the Dental Office

Next, here's a synopsis of each book. Sample chapters of each one are available at http://www.drsharonmitchell.org.

SYNOPSIS OF NOVELS IN THE AUTISM SCHOOL DAZE SERIES

Autism Goes to School

A single dad. An autistic child. A dedicated teacher. Can they be what each other needs?

After suddenly receiving custody of his five-year-old son, Ben must learn how to be a dad. The fact that he'd even fathered a child was news to him. Not only does this mean restructuring his sixty-hour workweek and becoming responsible for another human being, but also Kyle has an autism diagnosis.

Enter the school system and a shaky beginning. Under the guidance of a gifted teacher, Ben and Kyle take tentative steps to becoming father and son.

Teacher Melanie Nicols sees Ben as a deadbeat dad, but grudgingly comes to admire how he hangs in, determined to learn for his son's sake. Her admiration grows to more as father and son come to rely on Melanie being a part of their lives.

When parents receive the news that their child has autism, they spend countless hours researching the subject, usually at night, after an exhausting day. Teachers, when they hear that they'll have a student with an autism spectrum disorder, also try to learn as much as they can. This novel was written for such parents and teachers - an entertaining read that offers information on autism and strategies that work.

Get it free at https://dl.bookfunnel.com/k5ooc5awtp

Autism Runs Away

An autistic child flees in panic. The school can no longer cope. A mom at her wit's end.

Can Sara trust these strangers to look after her son, just one small child among hundreds, when he has ran from his own parents so very many times? She is about to find out. Is it worth the risk?

Ethan is only in grade one and already has been kicked out of one school due to his tantrums and pattern of running away when in a panic. Now, his mom's enrolled him in a new school but remains glued to her phone, waiting for the call to tell her to come pick him up, that they can't handle him, that they don't know what to do with a child who has autism.

Rather than attaching an adult to his side to keep him safe, this new teacher talks about calming strategies and choices. Do they not realize what could happen if Ethan flees the building? The impact of a car on one small body?

Sara is about to learn if this new school is up to the challenge.

Buy now to find out.Meet Kyle, Mel, Ben and the other characters you got to know in the award-winning bestseller *Autism Goes to School*. See what they've been up to in the last year and how they join forces to help Ethan.

Then, return to Madson School to see if Manny, a child with severe autism belongs in their midst. Read Manny's story in *Autism Belongs.*

Autism Runs Away on Amazon. Free with your Kindle Unlimited subscription.

Autism Belongs

A frustrated child. No way to communication. His aggression boils over.

Manny is not like other children. He doesn't talk. He doesn't leave the house. His parents desperately try to arrange their world so that Manny does not get upset. Because, when he does, well, the aggression was getting worse. Too many times Tomas had to leave work to rescue his wife from the havoc of their son's meltdowns. At ten, Manny was becoming difficult to handle.

Passing by a bakery made all the difference. There, they met people who understand autism, along with its strengths and challenges. They learn ways to help Manny communicate and socialize and to have his needs met.

Dare they consider letting him go to school? Is there a chance that Manny actually belongs there? You bet.

Meet Kyle, Ben, Mel and the other characters you read about in the Amazon bestseller *Autism Goes to School* and see how they've grown and progressed.

Buy *Autism Belongs* on Amazon or read free with your Kindle Unlimited subscription.

Autism Talks and Talks

Karen is bright, vivacious and highly verbal. Perhaps too verbal. She finds certain topics fascinating and goes on and on and on not realizing she has bored her audience. She remains on the fringe, looking at other adolescents having fun together and wondering if she could ever be a part of the group. Karen has **Asperger's Syndrome**.

Who best to help her but an **autistic chef**? *What?!*

Yep! Meet Jeff. His special talents and view of the world are just what Karen needs. And, Jeff learns that he is just what one particular woman needs as well.

Is this all there is for Karen? Will an autistic man find the love he didn't know he was seeking? Come join us and see.

Buy *Autism Talks and Talks* on Amazon or read free with your Kindle Unlimited subscription.

Autism Grows Up

An isolated young woman. Her frightened mom. A world closing in on them.

At twenty-one, Suzie has withdrawn from a world she finds alien and confusing. She has Asperger's Syndrome and high anxiety. To her, the world is a harsh, scary place where she does not fit in.

She spends much of her day sleeping and most of her nights on the computer. Her mother, Amanda, wishes Suzie would get a job, go to school or at least help out around the house. Suzie feels that her time is amply filled with the compelling world lurking within her computer.

Amanda wants more for Suzie, but does not know how to help her move forward. When she tries putting pressure on her, Suzie's paralyzing anxiety takes over, resulting in morose withdrawal or worse, lengthy tantrums.

Suzie is most content when alone in the basement with her computer. Staring at her monitor, the rest of the world falls away and she feels at home.

Amanda is torn. She met this gentleman, Jack. It would be nice to spend time with someone other than her brother and daughter but Suzie wouldn't like it and she needs her mother desperately. Jack gently persists and Amanda glimpses what her life could be like.

Uncomfortable questions arise like what will become of Suzie if something happens to Amanda? But when an intruder breaks into the house, Amanda has only Suzie to rely on.

Is Suzie up to the task?

Buy now to find out. Find it on Amazon or read free with your Kindle Unlimited subscription.

Autism Goes to School
Autism Runs Away
Autism Belong
Autism Talks and Talks
Autism Grows Up
Autism Goes to College
Autism Box Set
Autism Questions Parents Ask & the Answers They Need
Autism Questions Teachers Ask & the Answers They Need
As an Amazon Associate, I earn from qualifying purchases

Coming soon:

Autism and the Dental Office
The Autism Goes to School Workbook (Companion Workbook for Autism Goes to School

www.ingramcontent.com/pod-product-compliance
Lightning Source LLC
Chambersburg PA
CBHW020523080526
44583CB00013B/720